RUNNING WITH GOD

RUNNING WITH GOD

100 Day Devotional

ALEX BLACKBURN

Alex Blackburn

Contents

Dedication   xii

  1   Hide and Seek   1

  2   Though the Vision Tarries   3

  3   Jump!   5

  4   Silent Season   7

  5   Holy Spirit Speak   10

  6   Holy Spirit Power!   12

  7   My Body Is a Temple   14

  8   My Body Is a Temple 2   16

  9   Bring on the Rain   18

10   Through Hell and Back   20

11   Shine On!   22

12   Are We There Yet?   24

13   Dime a Dozen   26

14   Know Your Why   28

15 Learning the Hard Way   30

16 Everything That Glitters   32

17 Why Not Now?   34

18 Rainbow on the Other Side   36

19 Clean it Out   38

20 Surrender   40

21 Battle Weary   42

22 Prone to Worry   44

23 Faith is More Than a Feeling   46

24 Friend or Foe?   48

25 Rise above the Hate   50

26 Fear is a Liar   52

27 Death To Comparison   54

28 Shut the Door Behind You   56

29 Ready Set Go!   58

30 Trust the Process   60

31 Bold like A Lion   62

32 Chosen For Such a Time as This   64

33 You Are Not Done Yet   66

34 Give us Lord our Daily Bread   68

35 Rose-Colored Glasses   70

36 What Looked Like a Loss, Was a GAIN   72

37 Wanderlust   74

38 Fork in The Road   76

39 Are You Still Drinking from the Milk Carton?   79

40 On E...Time to Refuel   82

41 Let Go of the Wheel   84

42 All Other Ground Is Sinking Sand   86

43 Waves of Mercy   89

44 Go and Do All That is in Your Heart   91

45 Time is Passing   93

46 You are Not the Sum of Your Failures   95

47 Greedy Giver   97

48 Forward Thinking   99

49 Fortitude   102

50 Journey of Refinement   104

51 It Starts with You   107

52 Everyone Needs an Alexa!   109

53 The Attitude of Gratitude   112

54 Shake Off the Dead Weight   114

55 Pride Comes Before the Fall   116

56 Fast to go Far   118

57	Fasting is a Discipline	121
58	Say Hi!	123
59	Speak to the Wind	125
60	The Road to Consistency	127
61	Throw Away Your Expectations	129
62	Press On	131
63	What is the Meaning of Life?	133
64	Course Correction	135
65	Count The Cost	137
66	Silence the Voice of Doubt	139
67	Faith Killers	141
68	Shine Bright	143
69	Don't be a Chatty Kathy	145
70	Catch Those Judgmental Thoughts!	147
71	Offence is a Fence	149
72	What If?	151
73	Bending Over Backwards	153
74	Chasing Diamonds	155
75	Develop In Me A Willing Spirit	157
76	Harsh Reality	159
77	Victim or Victor?	161

78   He is Worthy To Be Praised   163

79   "Vengeance is Mine"   165

80   Create in Me A Clean Heart   167

81   Good Shepherd   169

82   Communication Error   171

83   Partnering With God   173

84   The Friend of God   175

85   Exercise It!   177

86   Be Plugged In   179

87   Church Hurt   182

88   Dig Up Those Talents!   185

89   Liar, Liar Pants on Fire!   187

90   Mighty Mountain Mover   189

91   Bride Of Christ   191

92   Keys to The Kingdom   193

93   The Freedom of Christ   195

94   A New Day Dawning   197

95   Receive The Good Gifts   199

96   Get Back Up Again   201

97   Juxtaposition   203

98   Be Like a Child   205

99 The Torch is Yours 207

100 Running With God 210

Have you accepted Jesus Christ as your Savior? 212

About The Author 214

THIS BOOK IS DEDICATED TO:

My beautiful daughter, Maliyah. May you always make Jesus the Lord of your life. I pray that you never put any limitations on what God wants to do in your life.

God sent me you in order to turn my life around. You're my angel. For you, I couldn't be more thankful.

My mother, Amy. I love you. It is because of you that I am able to dream big. As a little girl, you encouraged my "big dreams" and made me feel that anything is possible for me to accomplish! You have always believed in me, even when others haven't. Any time I share vision with you, I know that I can depend on you to cheer me on.

My nana in heaven, Linda, and my poppie, Ronnie. Thank you for raising me and loving me. Thank you for bringing me up in church. It's those seeds that were planted that brought me back to Jesus after a long period of rebellion. "Train up a child in the way he should go: and when he is old, he will not depart from it." Proverbs 22:6.

I

Hide and Seek

> *Ask, and it will be given to you. Seek, and you will find. Knock, and the door will be opened to you. Matthew 7:7*

As a little girl, one of my favorite games to play was hide and seek. I personally preferred to be the one doing the searching. It was always such an adrenaline rush to run through the house looking in every nook and cranny for the person hiding! It would spark feelings of excitement in me as I felt that I was getting closer to finding my friends that were hiding. Once I found who I was looking for, I would yell with joy and excitement, "GOTCHA!!!"

Think back to when you were a child. Did you enjoy playing a good game of hide and seek? Do you know who else enjoys playing hide and seek? God does!!

God chooses to hide sometimes because he wants us to

lean in and push into his presence until we find him. Until we find all of who he is. He wants to spark those feelings of excitement as we go deeper into the prayer closet to hear his voice and find his face. He gets very quiet like a good "hider" would do in order for his seeker to really pursue his presence. He desires us to seek him with all of our heart. Not just part of our heart, every single inch of it. Today, choose to be like a little child. Seek your father until you find Him.

2

Though the Vision Tarries

> *For the vision is yet for the appointed time, it testifies about the end and will not lie: though it delays, wait for it, since it will certainly come and not be late. Habakkuk 2:3*

Waiting can be really trying sometimes!! Waiting in lines, waiting for a promotion, waiting for a special phone call, waiting for an exciting event.... just to name a few. But there is something about waiting on God's promises that he has given you that can really test your patience on a whole 'nother level. What I am talking about here is that deep desire that he has deposited into your heart! The one that you know beyond a shadow of a doubt is a part of your future, but you do not see a single trace of it happening any time soon. Now that right there, can really test your patience and your faith!! Boy oh boy. Just talking about it makes me feel some type of way. But here is the thing...God is so magnificent in how he does things. He speaks promises into our lives, and for a while there will be no evidence of these things manifesting. But he does this, in order to test and build our faith and endurance.

What the Lord has spoken over you that you have yet to see, is a SEED! When a seed is planted underground, you cannot see it! You cannot see the roots beginning to form. But when it starts to sprout, yes, you see that! You get excited. Then it starts to grow and flourish! Just like God's promises over you! I want to let you know that you can go into your day knowing that if the Lord has promised certain things to you, they WILL come to pass. You may not see how, when, where, or why- but trust that God has a plan. His plan is to make it happen! Though the vision tarries, wait for it.

3

Jump!

> *Trust in the Lord with all your heart, and do not rely on your own understanding; in all your ways know him, and he will make your paths straight. Proverbs 3:5-6*

God is so interesting. He loves calling his children into deep waters. He loves watching us leap and soar to greater heights. If you feel in your heart that God is asking you to do something that is out of your nature and makes you feel uncomfortable, DO IT. You will be amazed at the outcome. True growth comes from leaps of faith. I can almost guarantee you that nine times out of ten when God asks you to jump into the unknown, you will have people that do not believe in you or tell you that it's not a good idea. Now, don't get me wrong, wise and Godly counsel is great...but when you know you're hearing from the Lord, you KNOW you are hearing from him.

We are not here on this earth to serve people but to serve our God. If he asks you to do something that doesn't make sense to anyone, take that as a honor and be obedient to your father. Just wait until you see what's on the other side of that big leap you take. You will be astounded, I promise. Do not be scared about falling, because God always honors an act of obedience. He will not allow you to crash and burn. This is the year to hold hands with your father and jump into the unknown.

4

Silent Season

But your iniquities have built barriers between you and your God, and your sins have made him hide his face from you so that he does not listen. Isaiah 59:2

I will give them a heart to know me, that I am the Lord. They will be my people, and I will be their God because they will return to me with all their heart. Jeremiah 24:7

I go through seasons of my life where I open up my Bible and I pray and I just don't really feel like I hear the Lord speaking. I feel like he's distant. Kind of goes back to when God plays hide and seek with us and he's wanting us to dig deeper into him so he can take us to higher levels in our faith.

Those seasons can be hard for me because I want to hear from him. I want those reminders that he is still there. I have learned over time that there are a few different reasons why we experience silent seasons. One of them being what I already mentioned: God calling us out into deeper relationship with him.

Another reason we may not be hearing the Lord is because God has given us a direction and we haven't been obedient to it yet. If this is the case, go and do what God told you to do!

If you have any unrepented sin in your life, this will separate you from the Lord and cause you to not hear his voice. Take some time to do some introspection, ask the Lord to reveal any unrepented sins in your life, and then repent to the Lord and follow him.

We may also be experiencing a silent season because we are not opening up our Bible to even hear the Lord speak to us. All good relationships require quality time to be spent with one another. What does your quality time with the Lord look like? Along with unrepented sin, lack of quality time tends to be a common reason for our generation to experience God's silence. People tend to get too distracted with their day to day life. It can be very hard to hear God when we are bogged down by the distractions surrounding us. Many of us have multiple roles we play in life and sometimes those things can take precedence over time with God if we don't have our priorities in order.

If you're experiencing a silent season, take some time to go deep into prayer today. Ask the Lord to open your ears to his voice and to quiet your heart, soul, and mind so you can hear him more clearly. Ask a friend to pray with you. Seek him and return to him if you've let your schedule get in the way of your time with God. If there is unrepented sin in your life, repent and return to him. Make God the first person you speak to in the morning. Prioritize him and everything in your life will fall into place. He will make time where it feels that there is no time.

5

Holy Spirit Speak

> *He says, "Be still, and know that I am God; I will be exalted among the nations, I will be exalted in the earth." Psalm 46:10*

Often, people can get confused with how to differentiate between God's voice and their own. God's word says that his sheep know his voice. Learning to hear God's voice, means that you must be spending time with him in the quiet place. The more you spend time with God, the more you will be able to identify your father's voice. Just like any other relationship, the more time you spend with someone, the easier it is to identify their voice if they are speaking and you're unable to physically see them.

What the Lord speaks to you will always be in alignment with his living and breathing word- the Bible. The Lord will never say something that is contrary to his word or contrary to his character. If you are unsure on how to hear from God, I will give you some tips. For those of you that hear from God well, I have something for you too, so keep reading!

For those of you learning to discern the Lord's voice: We've already covered that spending time with God daily is a must! You will need your bible, a journal, a pen, and a quiet place. You are going to designate a time every day, that you will sit before the Lord, pray, and ask him what he wants to speak to you. You will be still before the Lord and wait and listen. Anything that you hear, you are going to write down in your journal. The Lord will begin to confirm his words to you through scripture or through other people and he will help you see when you have heard him correctly. This is a practice! The deeper you dive into intimacy with Christ, the more you will be able to hear from him. Fasting is also another great tool to help fine tune your ears to hearing God's voice.

If you hear from the Father well, I want to challenge you to press in even deeper with him. Spend a longer amount of time in his presence than you normally do. If you spend 30 minutes with the Lord, shoot for 45 minutes. If you normally spend 45 minutes, then do an hour. It's amazing what all can unfold the longer we bask in God's presence. He loves spending time with you!

6

Holy Spirit Power!

> *Later he appeared to the eleven themselves as they were reclining at the table. He rebuked their unbelief and hardness of heart, because they did not believe those who saw him after he had risen. Then he said to them, "Go into all the world and preach the gospel to all creation. Whoever believes and is baptized will be saved, but whoever does not believe will be condemned. And these signs will accompany those who believe: In my name they will drive out demons; they will speak in new tongues; they will pick up snakes; if they should drink anything deadly, it will not harm them; they will lay hands on the sick, and they will get well. Mark 16:14-18*

When we ask God to live in our hearts, he deposits the holy spirit within us. This isn't just biblical lingo to make you feel official. This is legit. The power of God literally resides in your body. The same power that raised Jesus from the grave!

In scripture you will find that Jesus's disciples were able to perform miracles, heal the sick, drive out demons etc. It was not them doing these works, it was the power of God, the holy spirit, living inside of them.

You may wonder why you never hear about or see many people using these gifts. Unfortunately, some churches have chosen to dismiss the power of the holy spirit working through us, due to their own limiting faith or due to judgement from unbelievers. There are some people that also simply choose to not believe at all. If you do not have the faith for it, you will not see the fruit of it.

Go read 1st Corinthians chapter 12 to learn about the gifts of the spirit. I also suggest turning to the index in your bible and reading the scriptures that are beside of "holy spirit." Sit down with God and ask him to reveal what gifts he has implanted in you. Ask him to grow these spiritual gifts within you. To make a great impact in the world, and to truly be the body of believers that God has called us to be, we must have faith and yield to the power of God working through us.

7

My Body Is a Temple

Run from sexual sin! No other sin so clearly affects the body as this one does. For sexual immortality is a sin against your own body. Don't you realize that your body is the temple of the Holy Spirit, who lives in you and was given to you by God? You do not belong to yourself, for God bought you with a high price. So you must honor God with your body. 1 Corinthians 6:18-20

When the Lord lives within us, our body is truly a temple. A temple should be treated with care and respect. We shouldn't just give our body to anyone or anything. Our body is God's. It's important to know that when we say yes to the Lord, we are saying yes to the death of our old self. We must allow God to renew us from the inside out and make us more like him. Our desire to give our body away before marriage, or to engage in lustful thoughts, should begin to fade when we are seeking our father at a deeper level, because we will begin to have a deep desire to please him. Not because we're following a "law" but because of our affection towards him being so deep that our greatest desire is to please him. Because of our sinful nature, it can be really easy to mess up and fall back into old habits. If you fall, God has already given you grace, so repent and get back up again.

With the generation we live in, it can be really easy to fall back on the justification of: "everyone else does it." Or to have the mindset of: "that was then and this is now". But be reminded, God's word never changes. He wants his temple protected. He wants you protected. Who you were before God versus who are now, are two totally different people. You are not like "everybody else"- you are a child of the highest King. Cling to the cross; and the love of the father will pull you in closer and closer to him every time. You will have no choice but to give him all of your love and obedience because it will grow to become your deepest desire.

8

My Body Is a Temple 2

> *For drunkards and gluttons become poor, and drowsiness clothes them in rags. Proverbs 23:21*

This devotional is called "Running With God" because life with him is an adventurous run! Adventurous runs require a lot of energy! It can be very difficult to fulfill the calling and purpose in your life if you are constantly fatigued. The food and drink we choose to intake play a large roll in our energy levels. If you are more of a McDonald's, Burger King drive thru kind of person, would you say that after you eat those foods you feel like you could go run a race? I highly doubt it. I know I sure don't feel up to the challenge after stuffing my belly! I just want to take a nap! But God calls us to higher standards!

How are you fueling your tank? Your tank, being your body. Are you struggling with fatigue regularly? If so, take a look at your diet! If you want your energy to soar, change up your diet and get moving! Inactivity produces more inactivity. Action produces more action. We are movers for the Kingdom, so let's get moving!

I challenge you to seek healthier alternatives and to be more mindful about what you are putting into your temple. I also challenge you to begin some sort of fitness regimen if you don't already have one in place! Just a 30 minute walk a day can make the hugest difference in your life!

The greater you can function, the greater of an impact you can make. Each of us have calling and purpose that God has put on our lives, and the enemy wants to see us fail at every part of it. He wants us fatigued and lazy and unmotivated. Today is your day to fight back! From here on out, you choose health. One step at a time!

9

Bring on the Rain

> *Be glad, people of Zion, rejoice in the Lord your God, for he has given you the autumn rains because he is faithful. He sends you abundant showers, both autumn and spring rains, as before. Joel 2:23*

Do you ever experience times in your life where you feel, in the depths of your soul, that you are about to experience a shift? A shift into something greater? It seems like right before that shift occurs, circumstances can really beat you down. It feels like everything that could go wrong, starts to go wrong. But when this phase is over, all of the sudden blessings just pour out like rain on your head.

If you are currently going through a rough patch, put your faith in God and talk to him about your feelings. Ask God for his help. You're not meant to do this alone. And whatever you do, do NOT give up. Keep pushing. On the other side of this storm, is a rainbow. When I think of rain, I think of blessings pouring out on my head. Ask God to bring on the rain.

10

Through Hell and Back

> *Let us not grow weary in doing good, for at the proper time we will reap a harvest if we do not give up. Galatians 6:9*

Have you ever just had "one of those days!!" You know, one of those days where you wake up and start your day off with stubbing your toe against something and then you spill your fresh hot coffee on your brand new outfit on your way to work. Then at work, it becomes one thing after another. Then you leave and all you can think about is: "this was the worst day ever!" Um, yes, me too. Have you ever had a whole week like that? Or hey, maybe even a whole month or a few months where you just felt like everything that could go wrong, went wrong. Because believe me, I definitely have. But what's the point in that? If God loves us so much, then why would he allow us to endure such painful seasons in our life? What's the point in life kicking us down and shoving its elbow in our face 5 million times to leave us feeling battered, bruised, and at the point of no return? I'll gladly let you in on a little secret, it's for you to stand back up...EVERY SINGLE TIME.

Champions are those who continue to get up again and again, even after they've been knocked down countless times. It is in the fire that we are refined and where our character grows. It is also where we are able to see the goodness of God. God writes our testimony during these times. If you are going through a rough season, I want you to take a second to change your perspective. I want you to grab a sticky note and write "I AM A CHAMPION. I AM STRONG. I AM BRAVE. I CAN DO HARD THINGS". After you do that, I want you to go place it on your bathroom mirror. I want you to remind yourself every day that "this too shall pass".

Currently, God is writing a killer story through your pain that will soon turn to blessings! And you are going to be able to help many, many people who will go through the same struggles that you did. You are a walking testimony. Don't you forget that. There is light at the end of this tunnel. I can promise you that. ARISE CHAMPION!

11

Shine On!

For you were once in darkness, but now you are light in the Lord. Live as children of light. Ephesians 5:8

Hey, you!! Good morning. Or good afternoon... or good evening. Whatever is suitable for the time that you are reading this. ☺ Get ready for an awesome day! Do you want to know why today is so awesome. Well for one, because you woke up! You are breathing. Wow. That's quite impressive. Guess what that means? You have purpose!! Do you know what God says is the ultimate law?? LOVE. Yes, that's right, love! A huge part of your purpose is to walk in love.

How can you do that, you may ask? You can first start with loving yourself, your personality, and the body that God gave you. If you are prone to think negatively about yourself,

I want you to start each day with stating 5 things that either you love about yourself or things that you want to begin to believe about yourself. Even better, list 5 things that God says about you. For example- I am chosen. I am worthy. I am loved. I am courageous. I am beautiful. I am confident. I am a child of God.

It's amazing how powerful our words can be. Here are some other way's that you can walk in love: Take some time to send a gratitude text once a week to a friend, go through a drive thru and buy the persons meal that's behind you, or start up a conversation with a stranger and give them a listening ear and a smile. It's amazing how a smile will change someone's day.

Pray and ask God to give you an opportunity to make a difference in someone's life today. Did you know that God's children shine brightly?? Your smile can light up a room! From here on out, it's time to shine on!!!! Walk in your purpose and be love! Love shines brightly.

12

⚜

Are We There Yet?

> *For we walk by faith, not by sight. 2 Corinthians 5:7*

Read the title. What's the first thing that comes to mind? For me, the first thing I think of are kids in the backseat of the car, on their way to a vacation, asking for the 500th time, "are we there yet?" And by the 500th time, their parents are either ignoring them, yelling at them to hush, or answering them while simultaneously pulling their hair out.

Have you ever asked God that question? I have found myself asking him that question constantly. But I'm beginning to see that with God, it's never really about the destination. It's about the journey. It's about the things that we pick up and learn along the way. When we are constantly asking God that question, I believe he definitely gives us more grace than our parents did. But I also believe that at times God looks at us and says, "Oh, you of little faith.... Do you trust me??"

In all reality, if you've given your life to Christ, you've handed him the steering wheel. As long as you are being obedient to him, he's the one getting you to your destination. Do you trust who is behind the wheel? Do you trust the detours that he wants to take you on? Do you trust the unfamiliar roads with hills and valleys? Or are you going to continue to pester him with 'are we there yet?"

God knows we're human. He knows we are prone to doubt. But it is in the JOURNEY, that we grow into deeper intimacy with him, learn his character, and learn to truly trust solely in him: which is his ultimate goal. It is not by sight, but by faith, that we walk with him. So instead of asking "are we there yet" incessantly, it's time to start shouting "I'm ready for the ride Lord! Wherever you want to take me! I've got my seat belt on and I'm ready!"

13

Dime a Dozen

> *And God saw everything that he had made, and behold, it was very good. Genesis 1:31*

I'm certain you've heard of the phrase "dime a dozen." If you're referring to something being a "dime a dozen", this means that it is so plentiful as to be valueless. I'm here to remind you that you are not just a "dime a dozen." There is no one else in the world like you! You are a rarity. You are a ruby in a hidden cave! Hard to find but so precious and worthy!

Please remember how valuable you are. God chose you and crafted you just the way he did, for a specific purpose. He does not create just to create. He creates beauty and it has purpose.

Do not waste time belittling yourself. If you believe you

are "insignificant", you will start to sell yourself short. You will sell yourself short with relationships and with opportunities. You will believe the lie that you are not deemed as worthy enough to possess these things.

Beauty is in the eye of the beholder. The beholder is GOD and he deems you as beautiful and of the utmost value. You are worthy of all that and more. The kingdom is endless, and the kingdom is yours when you are in Christ.

14

Know Your Why

We can make our plans, but the Lord determines our steps. Proverbs 16:9

Take some time today to ask yourself why you do the things you do? What is it that you are working towards? Are the steps you're currently taking moving you closer towards your goals? It is vital that we have a clear knowing of our why. Or shall I say, a clear knowing of our WHO. If you ask most people who their "why" is, majority of the time they will speak of their family. But God is the ultimate "who" of the "why".

We should begin to centralize our focus on the biggest "who" there is: God. With him as our "why", we will not be led astray. We will be more motivated than ever, to accomplish every single task that he lays before us. We will be faithful to see all things to completion, because we know that we are doing it for a God that loves us and sent his son, our king Jesus, to die for us. We can never "pay" God back for all that he has done for us, but we can certainly devote our entire lives to serving him and following his every command. With keeping God first in your life, he will lay out each step before you and pave the way to every place he plans for your foot to step. The Lord says to run the race set out before us to obtain the prize. Keep your eyes on God and run until you obtain the prize because your "why" is waiting on who? You!

15

Learning the Hard Way

> *As for God, his way is perfect: The Lord's word is flawless; he shields all who take refuge in him. Psalm 18:30*
>
> *A wise son heeds his father's instruction, but a mocker does not respond to rebukes. Proverbs 13:1*
>
> *Blessed is the one whom God corrects; so do not despise the discipline of the Almighty. For he wounds, but he also binds up; he injures, but his hands also heal. Job 5:17-18*

I have always noticed that when you tell children no and they continue to rebel, nine times out of ten they end up getting hurt. I see it as God's way of showing them if they're not going to listen, then they will learn the hard way. Funny how we as adults tend to do the exact same thing.

We know within our heart of hearts that the Lord has told us that something is not for us, yet we want to rebel and find out on our own. The Lord is trying to save us from pain and regret but we want to take the longer and harder route just to see what may be on the other side. Curiosity killed the cat, I'm telling you!

I'm not sure why we choose to put ourselves through such troublesome moments. But hey, on the bright side, we learn. Even when we choose to learn the hard way! Learning the hard way definitely leaves an impact. It becomes an unforgettable moment. The pain of our own choices screams in our face and reminds us that our way is never the road we want to take! But thank God, his love comes rushing in to show us compassion and to teach us in love and truth.

The Lord wipes away our tears and teaches us that his way is always the best way. Today, choose to do things God's way. I promise you won't regret it. Yes, learning the hard way leaves a huge impact, but it's not necessary and it is painful. You can learn these things just by resting in God's love and seeing the blessings that come out of your obedience. Rebelling isn't the only precursor to learning a lesson.

16

Everything That Glitters

> *But test all things. Hold on to what is good. 1 Thessalonians 5:21*

Have you ever dated someone that was super good looking on the outside, but on the inside...they were lacking. They lacked compassion and maybe even had some egotistical or narcissistic tendencies.

Looks can be quite deceiving. We have to be careful to not allow our eyes to determine what is good for us. Because we all know the saying, "everything that glitters...isn't gold." This also applies to opportunities. Just because an opportunity looks absolutely perfect does not mean the opportunity is for you. Satan does this thing where he likes to dangle pretty things in front of our face to divert our attention and distract us. One of his main goals is to distract the Christian from the path that the Lord has set out before them. If he can get you distracted with the pretty things, he believes that he can get you to completely miss the beautiful and GOOD gifts that God has in store for you.

The "pretty things" that Satan dangles in your face are known as "counterfeits". They look like the real deal but they are fake! This is why growing in your discernment with the Lord is vital Just like a diamond expert can tell a fake diamond from a real diamond...you as a warrior Christian, should grow so much in the Lord, that you can discern a counterfeit when you see one!

Spend time with the Lord and read his word. The more you spend time with God and learn to listen to his voice, the more you will grow in discernment. The more you grow in discernment, the more you will be able to identify what is meant for you and what is only a distraction and trick from the enemy.

17

Why Not Now?

> *And the Lord answered me: "Write the vision; make it plain on tablets, so he may run who reads it." Habakkuk 2:2*

What are you waiting on? That idea that's been rolling around in your head but yet you haven't even put it from pen to paper. Come on. That's the first step! I know that timing is everything. But if you have a vision for something, you definitely need to put it onto paper now. The bible says that those with no vision, perish. Do you lack belief in your own self? Is that why you haven't written it down yet? Do you think that it's too hard and someone like you could never actually make that happen?

How about you stop feeding yourself those lies straight from the pits of hell! I want to encourage you today and let you in on something- NOTHING IS IMPOSSIBLE WITH GOD. If the Lord has put ideas in your heart and you partner with him, he will make sure they come to pass. You don't need to worry about a thing. You are the woman (or the man) for the job! So, why can't you start now?

A good starting place for you could be as simple as accepting the task and writing it down on paper. Then, going to the Lord to ask him for more of the blueprint/the plan. Write out a process for yourself on how you want to get this completed, what you need to get this completed, and when you would like to have it completed. There is no better time than now! People are waiting for your ideas! There are people that are waiting on your obedience. Get started!!!!

P.S. - As soon as you begin to doubt yourself, rebuke that lie. Speak out loud and say "I am more than a conqueror through Jesus Christ. My life is in his hands and the dreams and plans he has for me will come to pass. Satan, there is nothing you can do to stop the plans that the Lord has for me. You are a liar! In Jesus Name."

18

Rainbow on the Other Side

> *This is the day that the Lord has made; let us rejoice and be glad in it. Psalm 118:24*

One of the best things about rain, is when we're blessed to see a rainbow afterwards. They are so beautiful! Whatever you have endured in your past that left you feeling gloomy; it was just the rain your life needed in order to make a beautiful rainbow. I know those rainy seasons were, and are, hard. I know you felt like giving up many times. But it's always worth it. When you get to the place in your life where you are living in gratitude, that right there is the rainbow! Struggles teach us how to be content in all things. We must remember that there is always someone else that has it worse than us. It's a perspective change.

I know they say the rainbow is on the other side, but I think we can search for the beginning of the rainbow, even in the rain. The way that we can do this is by clinging onto God in our darkest moments. He is also our rainbow. I have had many days of crying in my living room floor and not thinking I can go on much longer. Crying from the depths of my soul, barely able to catch my breath. Feeling like my heart was absolutely crushed. Feeling like things would be easier if I were gone (sidenote: that is a LIE FROM HELL...if you have suicidal thoughts rebuke those thoughts in Jesus name!!!)

But during those crushing moments, God was speaking so clearly into my ear and holding me so tightly, that he was my rainbow in those dark and rainy seasons. He was my reason to keep going.

Another way that we can learn to see the rainbow in the dark is by beginning our day with journaling 5 things that you are grateful for. You can certainly find 5 things. Starting your day off with gratitude, even in those difficult seasons, can also be the start of your rainbow.

19

Clean it Out

I don't know about you but I cannot stand a cluttered area. It gives me anxiety and seriously stresses me out. I can't think straight in a cluttered area and if you're in a cluttered room... it's not like you can move about freely. Clutter usually means there's some kind of restraint. Clutter means there's not full access to that area. It's important that not just in our physical life that we are aware of clutter, but that were also aware of the clutter in our spiritual life.

One of the main things that can clutter our spirit, is unrepented sin! Clutter can also be old relationships that no longer belong in your life or it can be feelings like doubt/

worry/anxiety. Clutter in your spiritual life can be old mindsets that can't travel with you on this new journey. If you have any clutter in your spiritual home, it's time to clean it out!

For the new journey that you are going on, you can't take everything with you! It's easier to travel when you pack lightly (metaphorically speaking). Take some time today to self-reflect on what you need to clean out. Take some time this week to also declutter your home. Two reasons why you should do this: 1. Decluttering your home will help clear your mind and give you more peace. (it's really true!) 2. It's a prophetic act- showing that you are cleaning out the physical shows that you are ready to clean out the spiritual. It also shows that you trust that the Lord will help you clean out the spiritual. Go to the Lord and ask him what needs to be removed. Ask him to remove anything that does not belong in your life. When the Lord answers your prayers, please do not try and take anything back that he removes. He knows best. It's clean out time baby!

20

Surrender

> *The Lord will fight for you, you need only to be still. Exodus 14:14*

Fighting a losing battle is never any fun. It's quite awful really. I know for a fact every single one of us have experienced this. We're human and one of the most common "losing battles" that we try to fight is when we try to take the reins of our life and make our own decisions without partnering with God. Boy! Now that's a losing battle. Every. Single. Time. Hey, it may start off looking like you're doing a pretty swell job, and it may be enjoyable here and now. But it always, and I mean always, comes crashing down..quite traumatically to be honest.

The best thing that we can do when we are in the midst of this losing battle is to throw our hands up and surrender.

Surrender to the almighty king, God! He has your best interest in mind, and our God is a warrior. He wins every battle that he comes face to face with. There is nothing that is too hard for him and there is nothing that is impossible for him. If you choose to surrender to the Lord, you're always going to be on the winning team. There's no doubt about it. And it's funny, it may sometimes look like you're losing, but it never fails, you will always come out on top! Seriously! It's just how God works. He always makes a way in the wilderness. So, surrender child! You have been doing it your way for far too long. How well has that been working for you? Try God's way. I promise he won't let you down.

21

Battle Weary

> *A friend loves at all times, and a brother is born for a time of adversity. Proverbs 17:17*

Man. Reading this title alone takes me back to a dark place. The feelings of being "battle weary" are unexplainable. No energy to pray... and no energy to even cry. It feels cold and numb and frozen. Icky! Many of us will come into this place after we have gone through some intense spiritual warfare, or as the world likes to view it, some intense "everything in my life is going wrong no matter what I do" type of feelings. I recently experienced this. I had been warring in prayer for probably about 6 months and I was in this constant uphill downhill tango of things going great to things being horrible. I wasn't seeing the fullness of what God had promised me and it was extremely frustrating. I was honestly sick and tired of hearing reminders from the Lord about what he was going to do. Honestly, my attitude sucked. I had times of telling the Lord, "I genuinely just don't even want to hear it." I was struggling to read my bible and even hear from the Lord because I was shutting him out. I was tired of not seeing everything come to pass. That's not normal for me at all. This battle weariness lasted for about a week I believe.

I want to give you some advice on what to do when you come to this place. When you are in a place where you just feel numb to it all and you have no desire or energy to pray, FIND SOMEONE TO PRAY FOR YOU. Not just someone that says they are going to pray for you and then goes on about their business. But someone that will grab your hand or give you a phone call and pray with you in that moment. Prayer moves mountains. And there are times when we've been beaten down so badly that we don't have the energy for it- that's why God graced us with community. Humble yourself and reach out to someone that you know would be willing to pray for you and let them. And if you don't know anyone, ask the Lord to send someone to you that can pray for you and encourage you. He will.

22

Prone to Worry

Cast all your anxiety on him because he cares for you. 1 Peter 5:7

Why is it that us humans are so quick to go into worry mode? Like yo, where is your faith?? If we're not worrying about our family then we're worrying about our finances. If it's not our finances, then were worrying about what people think about us. It always has to be something! But does worry add anything to our lives? No, it only takes away. The Lord says to not spend one second worrying but to cast all of our anxiety onto him and to rest in him. Worrying comes from the root of fear. We are children of God and he has not called us to a spirit of fear but to a spirit of love, power, and of a sound mind. And we are going to choose a sound mind today and walk in it. We are going to walk hand in hand with the father and trust that he has every bit of our lives planned out and he is for us and not against us! Let me pray for you today:

"Heavenly Father, I bring this beautiful man/woman to you, and I ask that you would cover them in total and complete peace today Lord, I ask that if they are holding onto anything that does not serve them Lord, that they would loosen the grip and let go so they can rest in your perfect peace. I ask that you would remove that spirit of heaviness that is laying on them and replace it with your joy and your peace and your love. I ask that you would make them aware of anything that they need to repent for so that they can be near to you and hear you clearly. God, I ask that you would send them constant reminders of your love and of your goodness. Remind them that you are present and you are for them. Remind them that they are protected by you and that you have plans for their future, not plans to harm them. Surround them with your love today and every day Father. In Jesus Name, Amen."

23

Faith is More Than a Feeling

> *So then, just as you received Christ Je-sus as Lord, continue to live your lives in him, rooted and built up in him, strength-ened in the faith as you were taught, and overflowing with thankfulness. Colossians 2:6-7*

Faith is more than a feeling. Faith is a state of mind. Our feelings are fleeting. They're untrustworthy. They flip like a night switch. Switching on and off from good to bad and bad to good. If we choose to live a life based on our feelings, we will be all over the place, all of the time. Our feelings are impacted by hundreds (probably more) of stimuli a day. When we learn to live a life of faith, it grounds us. We can come face to face with adversity and acknowledge our feelings, and then follow them up with standing on the firm foundation of Christ.

We have to be careful that we are not putting the faith in ourselves but that we are putting our faith in God. God is our firm solid rock that we can stand on and our relationship with him is built on faith. When we become one with our father and learn his character by spending time with him, we learn how to live a faith filled life. If we don't spend time with God, then we can't fully trust him because we don't fully know Him.

The faith walk begins when you say yes to God and you begin talking to him and reading his living and breathing word. You will learn that he is the essence of faith and without him, we don't know how to truly faith walk. Faith is more than a feeling. Faith is a state of mind.

24

Friend or Foe?

> *He who walks with the wise grows wise, but a companion of fools suffers harms. Proverbs 13:20*

There is absolutely nothing better than being able to share your life with people that support you, love you, and are for you! Especially in this crazy world that we live in; friendship is vital. Being able to have a good and healthy support system is crucial. They said COVID was a pandemic...well loneliness, is an epidemic. But just because we're lonely, doesn't mean we can be close friends with just anyone! We must be wise in who we spend our time with. You may currently have people in your life that are "ride or die" friend's but there also may be some in your life that are wolves in sheep's clothing.

Now, not everyone has a deceiver in their friend group.

But I can almost guarantee that most of us have had a person like this in our lives at least once. It's really important that we are wise about the people that we choose to spend our time with. In some cases, you may have friends that are genuinely good people, but they may not necessarily be the best kind of people to be spending a large quantity of time with. When identifying if someone is a good friend to have around, there are some questions that you can ask yourself. Does this person motivate and uplift me or are they constantly gossiping about others and self-absorbed? When I leave this person, do I feel energized and filled with joy, or do I feel like the energy has been sucked out of me? Does this person care about my overall wellbeing, or are they just using me for their own personal agenda?

When choosing who we spend the most time with- we want to spend time with friends who push us to grow. Friends that are positive and genuinely love the Lord. Friends that won't sugarcoat the truth to you but will be real and upfront with you. Friends that won't allow you to make stupid decisions. The Lord has really blessed me this year with some real genuine friendships!!! Friends that go to war with me in the prayer closet. Friends that do not gossip and their utmost desire is to please the Lord. Now, that right there, is what you call a true friend!!!It doesn't get any better than God ordained friendships, okay!!

Ask the Lord to send you a tribe of "on-fire" believers to do life with! Also, ask the Lord to keep molding you and shaping you into a man/woman after God's own heart so you can also be the kind of friend that you are desiring!

25

Rise above the Hate

> *We love because he first loved us. 1 John 4:19*

It seems as if each day that passes, the world grows colder. At times it feels like the world is running on a short supply of love. If you turn on the tv, they are more likely to spend time talking about hate crimes than they are about people showing great acts of love. Don't get me wrong, awareness should be brought to the evil in this world. But we also should highlight the love in this world. Love overpowers darkness. Love is contagious. It's like a wildfire that spreads rapidly. If we would all do our part to show love to a stranger, we all could make this world a little brighter. I want to remind you today that although there is a lot of hate in this world, you can choose each day to rise above the hate and show love to a generation that needs it. Your simple act of generosity today or thought-fulness that you show someone, can go a long way. Like I said, Kindness and love will spread like a wildfire. The Lord wants you to play a role in showing this world what Christ's love looks like. The more you tap into God's love for you and you come to know him deeper and deeper, the deeper your love for people will grow. Ask God today for multiple opportunities to show his love to people that you encounter today. Be the spark that starts a wildfire in your community!

26

Fear is a Liar

> *We demolish arguments and every pretension that sets itself up against the knowledge of God, and we take captive every thought to make it obedient to Christ.*
> *2 Corinthians 10:3-4-5*

The enemy loves to see you cower and back down. His weapon is fear. "If I can cause them to fear, I can paralyze them. Then they won't fulfill their destiny." I imagine this is the thought process of Satan. Human tendency is to get caught up in the battle of our mind. We begin to let our mind play out scenarios of "what if's" and our thoughts begin to spiral. Before we know it, we have already concluded how the story will end before the story has even begun!

When we are faced with a situation that has an unknown

trajectory, we have to remind ourselves that we cannot write the story before it happens. We have to put a stop to our brain coming up with these outrageous stories of failure and embarrassment. 99% of the time, what you have imagined in your brain, is not how the story is going to play out. Our mind plays tricks on us all the time. Our mind is the enemy's favorite playground. He will feed your mind with lies if you let him. But what I am going to challenge you with today, is that every time you catch your brain trying to rationalize what will happen, stop yourself and give it to God. God says he will keep our mind in perfect peace! Your job is to walk through all situations with faith and know that God is going to work all things out accordingly.

27

Death To Comparison

> *You alone created my inner being. You knitted me together inside my mother. I will give thanks to you because I have been so amazingly and miraculously made. Your works are miraculous, and my soul is fully aware of this. Psalm 139:13-14*

Look friends, I am not a proponent of violence. But today, we are going to murder something! You and I, we are going to kill comparison!!!! Comparison is a joy stealer. Don't waste one second of your time comparing yourself to someone else. You and that person are on two totally different journeys. You have some amazing strengths and hidden talents, just as well as this person that you are comparing yourself to. You also have some weaknesses...but guess what, so does the person you are comparing yourself to.

I have found that many times, the person that you are spending time comparing yourself to is also comparing themselves to you. Taking time to compare your journey with someone else's, is an absolute waste of time. God is doing something completely different in your lives than he is in theirs. Don't you know that we were each made wonderfully and fearfully in the image of God? You are a unique masterpiece of the Lord We do not compare masterpieces because they each behold their own beauty!!!

28

Shut the Door Behind You

> As a dog returns to its vomit, so a fool repeats his folly.
> Proverbs 26:11
>
> Brothers and sisters, I do not consider myself yet to have taken hold of it. But one thing I do: forgetting what is behind and straining toward what is ahead. Philippians 3:13

Life is a series of open and closed doors. Especially when we surrender everything over to the Lord. There are some things that can't travel to each new season with us. There are doors that the Lord has to shut in order for new ones to open. God is a God of free will and choice so there are times where he will ask us to shut some doors in our lives. God doesn't say,

" Okay, *insert your name*, I want you to close that door but leave it cracked open just a bit, in case you start to miss it." God wants you to completely shut the door! Walk away from the door and don't you dare peek back inside!!!

God will not let you walk fully through the new door until you completely slam the old door shut. Ask yourself if you have any cracked open doors today? Are there any doors that you need to close completely? I know we may not know each other, but I do care about the wellness of your life. And I need you to know that if you are choosing to keep old options open when the Lord clearly wanted it removed from your life, it is only going to cause you harm and dismay. So please, quit the justifications, and shut the doors to the past. God is doing something new and he wants to swing some new doors wide open for you!

29

Ready Set Go!

> *Wait on the Lord: be of good courage, and he shall strengthen thine heart: wait, I say, on the Lord. Psalm 27:14*

When the Lord speaks "Ready set go" to you, you better get ready for the wildest ride of your life. God never does things in a small way! He is always full throttle and does exceedingly and abundantly more than we could think or imagine! But before the Lord speaks these words to you, he is going to take you through a preparation phase. This preparation phase looks a lot like the wilderness. Today we are going to refer to that wilderness as God's pause button. To you, it looks like your whole life is at a standstill but to the Lord, he knows what's really going down. During this time of bleakness, God is restoring you and preparing you for what is to come. Do not take this time lightly! Because it is detrimental to your success in the new that God is going to bring you. Be patient and do not grow weary in doing good because in due time you will reap a harvest! That's what the word says! It's all about perspective. View this time as your time of resting in the Lord and being still and waiting on him. Because once he says the words "ready set go!", he has already pressed the play button! You better be ready for some full throttle action!

30

Trust the Process

> *Who has ever heard of such things? Who has ever seen things like this? Can a country be born in a day or a nation be brought forth in a moment? Yet no sooner is Zion in labor than she gives birth to her children. "Do I bring to the moment of birth and not give delivery?" says the Lord. "Do I close up the womb when I bring to delivery?" says your God. Isaiah 66:8-9*

You know the saying, "good things take time"? How about this one:"Rome wasn't built in a day"? These quotes hit the nail on the wagon. God is a God of order and with order comes process. And if you haven't figured it out by now; the process isn't pretty! The purpose of the process is to birth new things in you in order to bring things to completion and for Gods plans and purposes to prevail. If you're a woman reading this- you know that birthing is definitely painful! Therefore, in the "process' of God birthing something new, it is natural for you to experience some "birthing pains."

God is so faithful during these pushing and trying times of our lives. He will send "midwives" (people to encourage you and speak life to you while you're birthing these new things) to help you birth these babies out! And just like when a woman is pregnant and goes through stages of her pregnancy- you will also go through stages in your process of birthing. Some periods will be really painful and others will be somewhat comfortable. You'll experience moments where you feel you have the hang of things and other moments where you feel that you just cannot take anymore! But once it comes time for you to actually give birth to this "baby", that's when the pressure starts to really build up!

I want to encourage you today by letting you know that if the pain is getting so difficult that you can hardly bear it, know that YOU ARE ABOUT TO GIVE BIRTH to the new things that God has in store for you!!! Get excited! The process is ALWAYS worth it because it always births NEW.

31

Bold like A Lion

> *Since we have such a hope, we are very bold. 2 Corinthians 3:12*
>
> *For God has not given us a spirit of fear, but of power and of love and of a sound mind. Therefore do not be ashamed of the testimony of our Lord. 2 Timothy 1:7-8*

My prayer for you today is that God makes you fearless and bold like a lion! Walking with Christ means walking by faith. And I pray that day by day your faith is strengthened by him. The more you spend time with the Lord by praying and reading his word, the more attune you will become to knowing his voice. God is always speaking if we keep our ears open to heaven. I have learned the more that we hear his voice and are obedient to it, the clearer and more present his voice becomes.

God has a mission for each and every one of us daily. But the question is, will you hear and obey? That's why it is important for us to keep our ears open. This requires a ton of faith! Because trust and believe, when the holy spirit whispers something random to you and asks you to go start a conversation with a stranger or tells you to pray over a person you just met... it takes a lot of courage, boldness, and faith to step out and trust and believe that you heard from the Lord. It's something that has to be exercised! But it is a million times worth it! Go out and live COURAGEOUSLY! Practice being obedient to the heeding of the holy spirit. It never feels good to regret the things you never said! Let's leave that regret at the door and speak what God tells us to speak!

32

Chosen For Such a Time
as This

> *And who knows but that you have come to your royal position for such a time as this?* Esther 4:14
>
> *For you are a people holy to the Lord your God, and the Lord has chosen you to be a people for his treasured possession, out of all the peoples who are on the face of the earth.* Deuteronomy 14:2

When you were younger, did you ever feel left out? Even as an adult, we can still experience moments where we feel left out. There may be times where we feel like we are not chosen by the people that we choose. Thankfully, that's not the case with God. He CHOSE you first. Before God put you inside of your mother's belly, He already had everything planned and mapped out for you. He had purpose written all over you. Purpose that screams "You are chosen!" There are many moments in life when God will present you with opportunities and you may feel unqualified or feel that you are not worthy of the calling...but God does not call the qualified. He qualifies the called! You were chosen for such a time as this!

33

You Are Not Done Yet

> *We can make our plans, but the Lord determines our steps. Proverbs 16:9*

You can plan your day, but God can flip that upside down. You can try and plan your life...but God can definitely flip that all the way around and back again. Sometimes we can get so caught up in our own plans that we are not even looking up to see if we are in alignment with where God wants us. We haven't taken the time to spend time with him to seek him out on the matters of our life. We can get so mixed up in trying to run our own lives that frustration starts to set in when things aren't playing out like we planned. But that's the thing with YOUR plan, YOUR plan might not always be God's plan.

Today, you may need the reminder that although things

look perplexing, and you feel that you can't tell your right from your left or your up from your down...God is saying to you today "YOU ARE NOT DONE YET!" What this means is, stop your worrying, and talk with your Father and tell him you want HIS will for your life. Just because you've gotten mixed up in trying to run your own life, doesn't mean that you can't get right back on track with making God, LORD of your life. That means surrendering your plans and your schedule to him because he is faithful to clean up your mess! And of course, if you are in a mess and the Lord is telling you "you are not done yet"... that means that you haven't completely annihilated every faucet of your life to where it's irrecoverable! You've got more life to live and more work to do- this time it's just going to be in alignment with what God is wanting you to do!

34

Give us Lord our Daily Bread

> *Now there is great gain in godliness with contentment, for we brought nothing into the world, and we cannot take anything out of the world. But if we have food and clothing, with these we will be content.*
> *1 Timothy 6:6-8*

In Exodus, after the Lord had set the Israelites free, they traveled through the wilderness for 40 years (should have been a shorter trip but their disobedience stretched the time). During their time in the wilderness, they spent the majority of the time complaining and wanting to return to a place that they were enslaved in because it was "easier."

After their complaining, God rains down manna from the

heavens and sends quail to their camp to provide for the Israelites and satisfy their hunger. What's interesting is that the Israelites persisted to complain to the Lord even WHILE he was meeting their need! The Israelites just were not satisfied. Their dissatisfaction very much displeased God.

God is moved by faith and gratefulness. God is more likely to give to those of us who are grateful for what we receive. Sometimes we can get so used to life being a certain way that we can start to become ungrateful for what we have. We get caught up in this 'More! More! More!" mentality. Similar to a toddler that's throwing a temper tantrum because his favorite cereal doesn't have the right amount of milk in it to give it that perfect flavor that makes his taste buds tingle! Quite ridiculous when you compare it to something like that... but that's what it looks like to the Lord. There is absolutely nothing wrong with asking God for bigger and better, but it definitely becomes a problem when you are crying and begging God to give you better and you're completely ungrateful and dissatisfied with what he's already given you. From prior experience, when I've cried out to the Lord for better, he didn't give me better until my heart posture changed from a posture of dissatisfaction to a posture of gratefulness.

35

Rose-Colored Glasses

> *I have learned the secret of being content in any and every situation, whether well fed or hungry, whether living in plenty or in want. I can do all this through him who gives me strength. Philippians 4:11-13*

When you hear the saying "She looks at the world through rose colored glasses," people can view that in two different perspectives. To some people, they would see that as a positive trait. To others, they would consider it disillusionment at its finest. To God, I believe he desires to give his children their own spiritual pair of rose-colored glasses in order for them to see people how he sees them and also for them to be able to live their lives in pure joy even amidst poor circumstances. Now don't get me wrong, the Lord gives us instruction to guard our hearts and to be wise. But I believe we can live life at a happy medium by using our Godly wisdom while walking with our spiritual rose-colored glasses on: seeing the best in people and loving them at their worst, just like Jesus.

Love is the activator to change. God also desires us to get to a place in him where we can learn to be happy under all circumstances, just like Peter said he learned to be! But how is it that we learn to walk with spiritual rose-colored glasses on? We learn this through spending time with the Lord and reading his word. If you can make that a daily practice, God will teach you how to view every circumstance from a place of victory and he will place those glasses right on your pretty (or handsome) little face!

36

~~⁓⚬⚬⚬~~

What Looked Like a
Loss, Was a GAIN

*After she had shut the door behind her
and her sons, they kept bringing her con-
tainers, and she kept pouring. When they
were full, she said to her son, "Bring me
another container." But he replied, "there
aren't any more." Then the oil stopped.
She went and told the man of God, and he
said, "Go sell the oil and pay your debt;
you and your sons can live on the rest." 2
Kings 4:5-7*

In 2 Kings, there is a woman whose husband had just
died and the creditors were coming to take her two sons

and enslave them because she didn't have the provision she needed. The only thing she had was just one small jar of oil. Little did she know, a lot can go a long way with the God of provision.

This woman ends up meeting a man of God named Elisha. He teaches her that what looked like a loss, was a tremendous gain. Although this lady didn't have much to give, she had everything to gain. Elisha gives her the instruction to go and borrow as many jars as she can find. With obedience, she goes out and gets as many jars as she can locate.

When the woman arrives back home with her jars, she takes the one "seemingly small" jar of oil and she begins to pour this tiny amount of oil into many, many, many jars. There was an abundance of it! This woman's "lack" gave room for a major gain! She was able to take these jars of oil, sell them, pay off her debt, and have oil left over for her and her sons to live on the rest.

Reflect on your own life. In the past, maybe even now, or in the future; you may experience a period of lack. But I want to tell you that if you are lacking something, praise God! Because you now have room to receive a mighty miracle of abundance from God. God will not allow his children to live in lack for a terribly long amount of time, God is a miracle worker and he shows up right on time! Every void place in your life, will be filled and overflowing with God's goodness.

37

Wanderlust

> *And he said, my presence will go with you, and I will give you rest. Exodus 33:14*

Is it bad that I had no idea what wanderlust meant until I just now googled it. I asked the Lord to give me a title name and here we are- wanderlust. Wanderlust means "a strong desire to travel". When you travel, you are going on a journey. I want to come at this from a symbolic point of view if you can follow my drift. With the word wanderlust, we are speaking about someone who loves to go on physical journeys. What I want to speak on in today's devotion is a person with a spiritual wanderlust! This would be someone who has a strong desire to journey with the Lord- any time, any place, any where. If you can position your heart to be in a place of wanderlust with the Lord, oh the places you will go! When you go on a journey, you experience new people, new places, new things, and ADVENTURE! Today I want to encourage you to tell the Lord that you want to have a spiritual wander-lust! You want to go on adventure with him. But just know that when you express this desire to the Lord, you better be ready to GO FAR'

38

Fork in The Road

He will not let your foot slip-he who watches over you will not slumber. Psalm 121:3

If any of you lacks wisdom, let him ask God, who gives generously to all without reproach, and it will be given him. James 1:5

Where would you be now if you would have never made the decisions that you did in the past? A lot of us like to think back on past decisions (good and bad) and ponder on how life would look differently if we would have never made the decisions that we did. It doesn't always take big decisions to make the biggest impact. The small daily decisions we make can make a huge impact on how the course of our lives will run.

I am so thankful that God's word teaches us that he guides the steps of the righteous and he will not let our feet slip. I don't know about you, but when I am faced with multiple options, it can be difficult to choose what is best. Sometimes you may only be presented with one option and it looks pretty good... but it might not be what's BEST for you. There are good things and then there are GOD things. We want to always choose the God things!

This is why our Godly discernment is key. We must seek the Lord on every faucet of our life. On the small decisions and on the big decisions. We also must utilize our faith in knowing that if we come before God with an upright and humble heart, that he will be certain to redirect our feet to align with his path. Life choices can be difficult to make and it can be hard when we feel that we need an answer right in that moment.

I've come to learn over the years that God is so faithful and that his answers come with patience, trust, and faith. If you just get quiet before God and spend time with him, you will learn his character. Not only will you learn his character, but he will also speak promises over your life. Make sure you are writing those promises down. These promises are going to be golden reminders in the times that you are faced with opportunities or faced with entering new relationships. You will be able to take what is presented to you and use God's magnifying glass to see if it lines up with what he has spoken over you. If it does not, then we already know to throw it out!

Now mind you, sometimes he may give you opportunities that don't look anything like they're connected to your promises, but they are just detours for training! So again, this is where wisdom and discernment is necessary!

Take your time when making decisions and always lay them on God's altar. Any path that doesn't lead to where God has already gone before you, is a path filled with consequences and burdens that you cannot carry. Follow the promptings of the holy spirit so you can continue walking in His freedom and security. Choose wisely.

39

Are You Still Drinking
from the Milk Carton?

> *But I, brothers, could not address you as spiritual people, but as people of the flesh, as infants in Christ. I fed you with milk, not solid food, for you were not ready for it. And even now you are not yet ready, for you are still of the flesh. For while there is jealousy and strife among you, are you not of the flesh and behaving only in a human way? 1 Corinthians 3:1-3*

God's goal for you is to go from drinking milk to eating solid foods. Drinking milk symbolizes you being a baby Christian (new to the faith.) You're still trying to figure out how to go from crawling to walking. Eating solid food symbolizes walking in the spirit and using your authority in Christ as a mature Christian would. God loves to accelerate this process when you are willing. Because here is the thing... once you say yes to Christ, the holy spirit is made readily available to you and everything that comes with it. God does not desire that you continue to turn back to your selfish ways. Every time that you continue to walk in flesh rather than grow in spirit, you are still metaphorically drinking out of the milk carton.

I don't know about you but if we're speaking realistically here, as an adult, I'm dang glad that I get to enjoy solid food! How unpleasant would it be to spend all of the years of my life ONLY drinking milk and never getting to taste the delightfulness of food? That sounds absolutely dreadful. Unfortunately, that's what some people continue doing. They keep sipping on the carton because it is more comfortable for their flesh. But God's plan for us when we said yes to him was that our flesh died with Christ and we were born again as a new creation in Christ walking in the spirit.

If you are reading this and you are feeling that you are still sipping out of the carton, GOD IS CALLING YOU HIGHER. It is now time for you to make the decision. God is asking you today, "Do you want to follow your fleshly desires and miss out on the fullness of what I have for you? Or do you want to be overwhelmed by all of the good things that I have for you when you say yes to walking fully in the spirit with me?"

Once you make this choice, this is when you begin actively pursuing Christ by reading his word and praying to him and being obedient to the instructions he gives you. The reason people stay drinking out of the milk carton is because they are not actively pursuing a relationship with God. God's kindness and his love is what leads us to repentance. His CHARACTER is what leads us to repentance. And you will never be able to see the absolute fullness of his character without spending time with him. Don't let God just be that one friend that you catch up with every 3 years and pick up where you left off... make God your ride or die that you can't go a day without speaking with! Allow him to show you the buffet of food he has waiting for you! Whether you realize it or not, your soul has been DYING to FEAST.

40

On E...Time to Refuel

> *In peace I will lie down and sleep, for you alone, Lord, make me dwell in safety.*
> *Psalm 4:8*

With the world we live in today, overworking yourself is seen as a trophy by some. Some people will parade about how busy they are. There are also some people that are terrified of rest. God is our commander in chief and he knows exactly what we need and when we need it. RESTING is very important!! First off, in Genesis, God takes 6 days out of the week to create the world. What does he do on the seventh day? He rests!! So rest, is an instruction from the Lord.

Rest is important for many reasons. Rest allows us to slow down and tune in deeper with God. It allows us to refuel for the week ahead and be the best that we can be for the next week! Rest also allows us to be very present in the moment with our family. Rest prevents us from burnout and it also keeps us healthy- physically, emotionally, and mentally. There are periods in life where God will call you to a complete rest that could last longer than a day. Resting for longer than a day can be more difficult for a lot of people and it requires a great amount of faith in knowing that God will take care of everything else while you are resting.

When God calls you to REST, it is very important that you are obedient to him and trust that he will be certain you will have everything you need. God can see the battles up ahead and he also knows if he's getting ready to throw you into something completely new that is going to require a whole lot of your energy. When we aren't obedient to the signs of us being called to a rest, sometimes God will physically make you rest through circumstances changing in your life that give you no other choice than to rest. A car can't go anywhere if it is sitting on empty, and neither can you! Make sure you are making time to let God refuel you.

41

Let Go of the Wheel

> *And he said to all, "If anyone would come after me, let him deny himself and take up his cross daily and follow me." Luke 9:23*

You might think you're a pretty good driver..but if we are talking about you having the wheel on your life, how's that been going for you? The best thing we can do is hand the wheel over to Jesus! The words the Lord spoke to me earlier today concerning this devotional was "let go of the "wheel" and let THY "will" be done." God's plans for you are far greater than where you could journey off to with just your hands on the wheel alone. Once we throw our hands up and say we are ready to hand the wheel on over to the Lord, that's when the ride of our life begins! When God takes the wheel, there are many unexpected twists and turns...but they all add up together to equate to the most thrilling and adrenaline pumping ride of your life! We can be so quick to want to maintain control on our lives, but in all reality, the tighter you grip the wheel, the more you begin to lose control! The tighter you hold on, the more difficult it will be for Gods plans to come to fruition in your life. You must loosen your grip, trust the one who created you, and hand the wheel over to him! Surrendering to God will take you further than you could ever imagine.

42

All Other Ground Is Sinking Sand

Everyone then who hears these words of mine and does them will be like a wise man who built his house on the rock. And the rain fell, and the floods came, and the winds blew and beat on that house, but it did not fall, because it had been founded on the rock. And everyone who hears these words of mine and does not do them will be like a foolish man who built his house on the sand. And the rain fell, and the floods came, and the winds blew and beat against that house, and it fell, and great was the fall of it. Matthew 7:24-27

Let's say you have plans to build a new home for you and your family. If you are given a choice to build your new house on a solid firm foundation or on sand...which groundwork would you be choosing? That's kind of stupid question, isn't it? In reality, no one would be stupid enough to even present the sand as a foundation for your new home. So why is it that we sometimes build our life on sand rather than on the firm solid rock that Jesus Christ is? I believe a lot of us have tried to do things our way in the past, and we start building our "homes" on things that will never last. We build on our reputation, on our ego, our position of power, relationships... But what happens to us when those things start to be shaken, when things fall out of order, when your removed from your position that you built your identity in, when that relationship ends... Your whole life comes crumbling down.

Everything that you took so long to built did not outlast the storm. If you built your "house" on your own, I am here to lovingly tell you- you're standing on shaky ground my beautiful friend. That foundation must crumble. When that foundation crumbles, or if it already has, PRAISE GOD! Because now, NOW, God is going to do a work in you that is going to blow your mind. God is giving you a clean slate and now it's your choice to hand over the tools to the best constructor in the WHOLE. WIDE. WORLD.

Let me tell you something, once you make the decision to give it over to the father and let him construct a new home for you- your foundation will NEVER be shaken. You will be built on the solid rock of Jesus Christ himself. Rain, hail, sleet, storm can come blowing your way- but you will be PLANTED and never uprooted! If your life is not built on Jesus, all other ground is sinking sand.

43

Waves of Mercy

> *Who is a God like you, who pardons sin and forgives the transgression of the remnant of his inheritance? You do not stay angry forever but delight to show mercy. Micah 7:18*

You know that feeling after you've done something you know you are not supposed to do? Most of us, want to hide after doing something we are ashamed of. Fear, shame, and guilt start to creep in. I believe that those feelings are healthy to feel for a moment. But by a moment, I mean, a SECOND. Those feelings make you aware that you have just done something to cause yourself, or someone else, harm. If it wasn't for our pain receptors, if you placed your hand on an oven, you would face detrimental trauma to your body. But thankfully, our body acknowledges when we have put it through harm.

Same thing goes for when you do something you shouldn't do, your emotions make you aware that it was not the best decision. But here's where we make use of those feelings- we take them and we immediately throw them to God and ask him to rid us of the shame, guilt, and fear.

We ask our Savior, to forgive us for our sins and we ask him for help to make better decisions from here on out. God is not a God of condemnation, but the God of conviction and forgiveness. Satan desires you to sit in self-pity, to isolate yourself from the world, and to mope around in your fear, shame, and guilt. God's desire is for his grace, love, and mercy to lead you to repentance. God's word says that where the spirit of the Lord is, there is freedom. God wants you to live in complete and utter freedom. God wants his mercy to wash over you like mighty rushing waves and to free you from condemnation. Acknowledge your guilt, but then give your worries to God and repent!!! Thank God for his waves of mercy today!!

44

Go and Do All That is in Your Heart

> *And Nathan said to the king, "Go, and do all that is in your heart, for the Lord is with you." 2 Samuel 7:3*

The only thing that is stopping you, is you. Now, listen, there is a time, place, and season for everything under the sun (Ecclesiastes tells us that.) But God will give you open windows of time where he will give you instruction and he is waiting on you to go out and follow through with what he has asked of you to do. Do not dismiss the seemingly small instructions he may give you. Do not despise small beginnings either! Because when God sees you being faithful with the humble beginnings, he is going to bless you with greater.

When God plants deep desires into your heart, they are there because he is showing you glimpses of what his plans are for you. But these desires will require your faith plus action in order to see the manifestation. No one else can thwart the plans that God has for your life- only your disobedience can!!! Keep your eyes focused on the gaze of Jesus and he will make your paths straight. Go and do all that is in your heart, because he is with you!!!

45

Time is Passing

> *Look carefully then how you walk, not as unwise but as wise, making the best use of the time, because the days are evil. Therefore, do not be foolish, but understand what the will of the Lord is. Ephesians 5:15-17*

As the hand continues to pass on the clock, time continues to pass us by. What are you doing with your time to make it of good value? Now please don't get in a tizzy and become worried that you are not doing enough. But, we also must really take the time for some deep introspection to make sure that we have been stewarding our time on earth well. The hugest piece of guidance I can give you here is to affirm you and let you know that if you have chosen to lay down your life, to pick up your cross, and follow Jesus- none of your time here on Earth will be wasted.

Following Jesus means doing things that push us past our fear and have us walking in faith. When we walk in faith, we are obedient to God's instruction. If we have ears inclined to hear our father and his instruction, we will never be led astray. Every piece of Gods story that he Has written for our lives, will play out as planned. But, it is also important that I mention, that some people say that they walk with Christ, yet they don't spend time reading his word and praying and they get caught up in their every day lives. This is when we can miss it. We can miss the heeding of the holy spirit instructing us. If we are too focused on being the God of our own lives, we will drown out the holy spirit and the calling that he has on our lives. The more time you spend with God, the more your faith will build, and fear will leave. The more you will know your father's voice; so when he calls you into deep waters- you will jump out and follow that call! Steward your time on Earth here well!!! As long as you give your heart to God and actively seek him, he will direct your paths and no time will go wasted!!

46

You are Not the Sum of Your Failures

> *So God created mankind in his own image, in the image of God he created them; male and female he created them.*
> *Genesis 1:27*

Psychology considers "identity" as the qualities, beliefs, personality, looks, and/or expressions that make a person. As a child, most of us allow the world to play a role in shaping our identity. A large part of our identity becomes a sum of the positive, as well as the negative comments that we received from others over the years. We take our wins and our losses and throw them into the mix as well. Typically, it seems that the negative beliefs we have of ourselves shout so much louder than the positive beliefs that we've formed over the years. If you were told you would never amount to anything in life, you may consider yourself as "unworthy." If you struggled to make good grades in school, you may view yourself as "stupid." If your parents abandoned you, you may see yourself as "unlovable." The list goes on.

This list, is a whole bunch of lies from the pits of hell. You are NOT the sum of your failures. God calls out our identity in the beginning of the bible, in Genesis, and says that we were created in the IMAGE of GOD. God says that when we profess Jesus Christ as our savior, we are a NEW creation in Him and all of the old passes away. God say's that when we say yes to Him- we are CHILDREN of GOD. Heirs to his throne. We are seated in heavenly places! This means you are ROYALTY. Royalty stands with it's head held high and can look in the mirror and say "My identity is in Christ! I am loved. I am enough. I am WORTHY. I am Chosen by King Jesus." If you struggle with your identity, my prayer for you is that you find it so deeply rooted in Christ that it can never be shaken again. Again, must I remind you; YOU ARE NOT THE SUM OF YOUR FAILURES.

47

Greedy Giver

> *Each man should give what he has de-cided in his heart to give, not reluctantly or under compulsion, for God loves a cheer-ful giver. 2 Corinthians 9:7*

God knows your motives. He knows every inch of your heart. Whether you say it out loud or not, God knows what your intentions are and why you do what you do. There are Gracious givers and greedy givers. Which one are you? A gracious giver is someone who gives eagerly without expect-ing anything in return- they have the heart of someone who genuinely wants to bless the other person.

A greedy giver, is someone who gives because it makes them feel good about THEMSELVES, or they hope to re-ceive something in return from the other person. God desires a heart that graciously gives their time and money. We all struggle with character defects because we were born into this world as humans that are prone to sin. But praise God, God can make us all brand new!

If you struggle with your heart's intentions leaning towards greed, pray and ask God to renew your heart and to make you a gracious and humble individual. Ask God to make you more like Jesus and remove any greed that is in your heart. For those of you that are graciously giving, God wants you to know how proud of you he is! He loves that you have a heart for people and he will continue to bless your giving because you give with such a loving heart. And another word of encouragement for those of you that felt convicted while reading- just repent, God forgives you. And He is going take that greed out of your heart! God is going to soften your heart more and more as the days pass by and you will be a humble hearted, gracious giver, that God is going to abundantly reward!!!

48

Forward Thinking

> *So I went down to the potter's house, and there he was working at his wheel. Jeremiah 18:3*

For those of us that consider ourselves "structured individuals", most of us sometimes have difficulty thinking outside of the box. I would consider myself a creative person, but I am also very structured. In the past, I would be so rigid with some of my thinking, that it would be difficult for me to step outside of my own box that I had created with my thinking. And oh boy! God did not let that character trait stick around for the rest of my life. God began throwing so many different wrenches my way to get me outside of my analytical mind. The Lord positioned me in a job working with children in occupational therapy for 2 years and the whole foundation of the job is...take a guess if you're unfamiliar with this line of work... it is THINKING OUTSIDE OF THE BOX.

Then, I started noticing that the Lord started inserting new relationships into my life. People who were constantly changing things up, always going with the flow, and were constantly reorganizing their areas (which were also areas that I shared with them.) When I say it drove me crazy, it drove me crazy!!! This will sound very odd, but it physically hurt me inside! It was like a scratch that I couldn't itch. But God knew exactly what I needed.

God also knows exactly what you need! If you struggle with being too analytical, when you choose to walk with God, he will shake your life up and start putting you into situations and surrounding you with people that are completely opposite! He will continue to do this until you begin to loosen your grip and now he has control. He will shape you and mold you just like clay.

Analytical minds are great! Creative minds are great! But what is even better, is when God teaches you to have the perfect balance of both! I believe God wants us all to be forward thinkers. A forward thinker is someone who has a nice balance of creative thinking and analytical thinking. After all, God is the most forward thinker in the whole universe and God's word says that we are made in his image- therefore, we must all have a forward thinker inside of us that just needs to be uncovered! Ask God today to uncover your inner "forward thinker." If you already consider yourself a forward thinker- ask God to uncover MORE. There is always MORE to you than you can see. Be open to God's hand moving in this area of your life.

Character traits of a forward-thinker: Open minded/open to change, creative and analytical balance, not dwelling in the past, visionary, thinking outside of the box, and fortitude.

49

Fortitude

> *Be strong and courageous; do not be frightened or dismayed, for the Lord your God is with you wherever you go. Joshua 1:9*

For the past two weeks the holy spirit has whispered the word "Fortitude" to me. This is slightly embarrassing, but I had to look up the definition. The definition of the word Fortitude is- "courage in pain and adversity." I kept wondering why he kept speaking the word to me and the Lord only wanted to reveal to me that he has built great depths of fortitude in me over the course of my life through the adversity that I have faced.

We need the stimulus of PAIN for GROWTH. When you first faced an adverse situation in your life, your courage may have been slim to none. But the more you come face to face with adversity, the thicker your skin becomes and the more you grow in courage. If you've been through some hard times or two, you know what I am speaking of!! It takes the pressure to form diamonds. If you are going through a difficult season in your life (or for future difficult situations you may endure), I want to encourage you by letting you know that God will use those difficulties to FORTIFY you!!!

50

Journey of Refinement

> *Now the Lord is the Spirit, and where the Spirit of the Lord is, there is freedom. And we, who with unveiled faces all reflect the Lord's glory, are being transformed into his likeness with ever-increasing glory, which comes from the Lord, who is the spirit. 2 Corinthians 3:17-18*

Rome wasn't built in a day. And neither are you. Walking with God is exactly what it sounds like. It is step by step with the father. Now, I understand the name of this devotional book is "Running with God" and that is because when we partner with walking with Christ, not only are we walking with Him, but we are running the race of our lives with Him as well.

But, back to the walking...God is going to work things out in you step by step. You don't just say yes to Jesus and then become a superhero Christian that lives out the holiest life in one day. It's a process. Refinement is a process. What refinement is, is God testing you and trying you like gold, in order to bring your impurities to the surface so that he can remove all impurities from your body. Those impurities are your sinful habits, thoughts/desires.

To share with you my own personal experience, my walk with God has been a great example of a JOURNEY of refinement. To give you a quick summed up timeline, I asked Jesus into my life at 8 years old and the older I became, I started living for the world and turning away from him. I struggled with addictions and finding love in the wrong places, then God gave me my daughter and he freed me from drugs. Soon after my daughter, I finally surrendered everything over to Christ. He then freed me from sexual immortality, he freed me from smoking addiction, and freed me from drinking/using alcohol as an escape and most recently he freed me from unforgiveness, bitterness, and lust. All of this refining the Lord has done in my life has been over the course of many, many years! And in between all of the refining, I made many, many, many mistakes! But, my heart was always going back to the father and my heart was genuine! I felt remorse for sinning against my father and my heart truly wanted to be holy and to follow him. I share this with you, so that you can know that if you are battling strongholds or addictions and you genuinely want to live for the Lord and you are seeking Him, He WILL set you free. He will, he will, he will. Freedom is your portion

51

It Starts with You

> We encouraged, comforted, and im-
> plored each of you to walk worthy of God,
> who calls you into his own kingdom and
> glory. 1 Thessalonians 2:12-13

Let's go get em tiger! It starts with you. You have the power to make decisions and choices that will lead you to greater things. With God as your GPS, all you need to do is make sure you have spoken to him and released all of your plans and desires to him. Ask him to replace your old desires with his desires and his plans for you.

God gives you the power to choose and to discern what is for you and what is not for you. This is why it is ultra important to stay divinely connected to the throne room of heaven. When you can come into agreement with who Christ says that you are and you surrender everything at the foot of the cross, you can start to make some headway.

When you can align every part of yourself to the Kingdom of God, you will begin to see things manifesting in your life like never before. Please don't think I mean just material things because God is far more concerned with other things in your life. You will begin to see an increase in joy, happiness, peace, and fulfillment. In addition to that, you will also see an increase in the material things as well. It all starts with you choosing alignment with God's kingdom.

5²

◈

Everyone Needs
an Alexa!

> *As iron sharpens iron, so one person sharpens another. Proverbs 27:17*

I'm going to share one of life's greatest gifts with you- it is the gift of Godly/covenant friendship! God created us for community. It is not good for man to be alone! When I say everyone needs an Alexa, I mean it!! No, I do not mean the Alexa that lives in your home; the one that you tell what to do and what song you want her to play etc. I understand some of you introverts may prefer to just chill with the robot (I can tend to also be said introvert!). But no, I mean a friend. A REAL friend!

The Lord has blessed me with this friendship I have found

in one of my beautiful friend's Alexa. When I say there is nothing like Godly friendship, there is nothing like it. Alexa is someone who has great faith, she is there when you need her, she gives Godly wisdom and counsel, she will tell you if you are treading on water that might not be the wisest of you to tread on, she will pray for you, she will fast with you, she will grow with you, and she will learn with you!

It's so interesting when God joins friendships together because he will highlight each of your strengths and weaknesses and allow one another to learn from the other. There will be similarities but also some differences! And the differences are probably the best part!

It's in the differences that we often see the most growth and how we can learn from this person. There is also nothing better than being friends with someone who is a prayer partner! They don't just say they are going to pray for you, they do it with you IN THE MOMENT.

Godly friendships can also have their uncomfortable and rocky parts too! God will use these covenant relationships to help strengthen one another and that, a lot of times, can be quite uncomfortable! There can be periods where you feel like you want to run, but that's probably because there is some healing taking place and that can also be uncomfortable! Satan wants to do his best to cause division. But God wants to allow certain things to rise up, in order to do deeper refining and growth in the two of you! Godly friendships will force you to have hard conversations which will force you to grow!

This, this, this...is a true friend. TRUE friendship is GODLY friendship. It is beautiful, wonderful, and such a blessing! Ask God to bring a friend like this into your life, if you do not have one. Someone that will pray, uplift, and speak the truth!

53

The Attitude of Gratitude

> *Rejoice always, pray without ceasing, give thanks in all circumstances, for this is the will of God in Christ Jesus for you. 1 Thessalonians 5:16-18*

I want to give y'all a tip for when you pray. Pray from a place of gratitude! Thank God in advance for everything you are asking him to do in your life. When you pray from a place of gratitude, you are praying in a place of great faith. Faith as small as a mustard seed will move mountains, so just think how this type of praying can change your prayer life, your life in general, as well as you! When you start to pray from a place of gratitude, you begin to retrain your mind to be in a constant place of gratitude. God's word says that his children lack NOT ONE good thing, therefore the outpouring of that should be gratitude no matter what it "looks like"! We need to be thanking God in advance for what we are praying for because it is on its way! Packaged however the Lord deems fit! It may not look like exactly what you prayed for, but you will come to find out that it is even better! And you will be thankful for it!

The attitude of gratitude is the best to have because it completely alters your whole being! You will be walking on clouds even in the storm if you can pray and live with an attitude of gratitude. Begin your prayers with thanking God for just who he is in general and how amazing he is. Then start thanking God for everything that is to be done in your life! Even thank him for the hard times, even in the midst of them, because whether you can see it in that moment or not, God is going to turn it all around for your good and he is growing you in that adversity! God's ready to hear those thank you's and see your faith in action!!!

54

Shake Off the Dead Weight

> *A good person produces good out of the good stored up in his heart. An evil person produces evil out of the evil stored up in his heart, for his mouth speaks from the overflow of the heart. Luke 6:45*

When someone wrongs you, it can be quick and easy to want to respond in the flesh. It can also feel easier to shove the problem down and ignore productive communication with the person that wronged you. If you make the decision to shove it down, ignore the problem, and hold a grievance towards this individual- you are holding onto dead weight!

Unforgiveness, bitterness, anger, hate... all of that, is dead weight. Imagine all of those feelings and emotions taking up space in your body. If you have held onto every wrong-doing that someone has committed against you, never letting it go...that is holding up a lot of empty space in your body! Those emotions do not give room for love to flow freely. God is love. This is why God instructs us to forgive others because he wants to move FREELY in your life, no restraints! And all of those negative emotions are restraints.

Praise God that he can break through our self-constructed restraints though, am I right?! When something is taking up a lot of space to where there's not much room left- those things must come out! So think about this, if you are holding onto all of these negative emotions, what do you think is going to come out of you? Would it predominately be war or peace? It's going to be war! You are going to be quicker to explosive anger than responding in a gentle nature...that's just the way it is! Ask the Lord to uncover the deadweight you are carry-ing! Ask him to break those restraints of unforgiveness and harboring of hate that have been in your heart. Ask the Lord to give you a heart that is clean and filled with the love of Jesus. You have so much more love to give!!!!

55

Pride Comes Before the Fall

> *But everything exposed by the light becomes visible- and everything that is illuminated becomes a light. Ephesians 5:13*
>
> *Pride goes before destruction, a haughty spirit before a fall. Proverbs 16:18*

You can spot a prideful individual from a mile away. But God can spot the individual that walks in false humility with pride residing in their heart. God see's what we cannot see. God's light shines down on darkness and he will be quick to reveal the truth in your life. The Lord was speaking to me today and he was saying to tell his people that he resists the proud! He said that the battle was not to the strong but to the humble. What He meant by this was that it isn't the strong that will win battles, it is those that are humble that will win battle after battle

He spoke the verse to me "In quietness and confidence shall be your strength." This means true strength is derived from a humble heart. I think everyone of us on this earth struggle with pride to at least some degree. In America, status is of great importance, and it is natural for us to have tendencies to lean towards being prideful given what us Americans deem as being "pride worthy." If we're living the "American Dream" we can be quick to carry some amount of pride.

Now don't get me wrong, you should be proud of your accomplishments ..but you should also be humble enough to know that you would have NOTHING or have accomplished nothing without God's grace and abounding love and mercy. Let me tell you something, if you are a follower of Christ, God will not allow you to settle in prideful ways. God is QUICK to humble those that are prideful. The humbling of Christ is definitely one of the most difficult processes to undergo but it is so necessary and so worth it. God will sit you down REAL QUICK and show you who your Lord is. You are not Lord over yourself or your possessions or your accomplishments, God is. If it wasn't for God, you wouldn't be where you are at today. Thank Him! If you struggle with pride, ask God to humble your heart. Again, the process is not easy, but it is worth it. God gives exceedingly and abundantly more to his humble hearted servants!

56

Fast to go Far

> *And Jesus, full of the holy spirit, returned from the Jordan and was led by the Spirit into the wilderness for forty days, being tempted by the devil. And he ate nothing during those days. And when they were ended, he was hungry. The devil said to him, "If you are the Son of God, command this stone to become bread." And Jesus answered him, "It is written, Man shall not live by bread alone." Luke 4:1-4*

If you are reading this devotional, then I could probably take a pretty good guess and assume that you have a desire to grow closer to God. Am I right? With that being said, there is a key to closeness with God that you are going to read about today! This key is called fasting!!! There are many categories that you could fall into here- 1. You've heard of fasting but have no idea how to do it. 2. You know about fasting, but you've never done it or have understood the importance of it. 3. "What the heck is fasting?!" or 4. You've fasted before and you know all about it!

No matter what category you fall into, finish this read today! Fasting is one of the number one ways to fine tune your ears to hear God's voice. If you want to hear the holy spirit more clearly, fast! If you want to deepen your relationship with God, fast! If you need a breakthrough in ANY area of your life, fast! If you need instructions and guidance from God, fast! If you need to see breakthrough in your loved ones life, fast!!!!! Fast. Fast. Fast. Do you get the gist of what I'm saying here? Fasting isn't an option in the Christian walk. It is expected of us! God calls us to fast because he wants us to live in the fullness of our spirit- it's for our benefit!

Now, for those of you in category 1 and probably category 2...the next question you are most likely thinking of is, "okay..so like..how does this work? How am I supposed to fast??" Let me tell you! There are different ways to fast but I'm going to only cover two different methods. They're pretty simple. There is a water fast- which involves only drinking water and no food and there is a partial fast- which is like intermittent fasting where you skip a meal or two.

In tomorrow's devotional, I will talk about what my journey of fasting has looked like which I think could be helpful for you if you are new to this. The first piece of advice I want to give you is to ask the holy spirit how long you should fast and how he wants you to fast. If you're uncertain as to how to hear the holy spirit, my suggestion to you is to plan in advance when you are going to fast and also be praying the week leading up to your fast asking God for help with this. If you're a beginner you may want to start out with a partial fast a couple of times before doing a full water fast. God will give you the strength for this! And I can promise you, fasting will help you go further in your walk with Christ! Fasting will increase your faith and you will begin to see more supernatural things in your life! It is worth it!!

57

Fasting is a Discipline

> *But I say walk by the spirit, and you will not carry out the desire of the flesh. For the flesh sets its desire against the Spirit, and the Spirit against the flesh; for these are in opposition to one another, so that you may not do the things that you please. Galatians 5:16-17*

Look, I don't know about you, but your girl loves to eat! I am a total foodie. I'm the kind of girl who will plan out my meals in advance and literally daydream about them during the week. When I learned that fasting was a spiritual discipline that I needed to start incorporating into my life, I was wondering how the heck am I going to do this?! I've always had a strength in bearing great faith, so I just told myself: "I will do this with God's strength, not my own." The very first time I fasted, I bought myself a Starbucks latte. That alone, was probably 600 calories. I continued to fast that way probably 4 or 5 more times. After that, I realized, I wasn't exactly making my flesh submit to the spirit by feeding it a 600 calorie coffee and needed to go without the coffee in the future and do a true/complete fast. It took multiple trials of fasting before I was able to go a full 24 hours with 0 calories in my body, I mean MANY multiple attempts. The longest I've been able to fast for now has been 70 hours.

I share all of this to say, fasting is a discipline! Give yourself grace. It takes time to build up your spirit man and to kill your flesh. You might have no problem jumping right in and doing a 3 day fast or even longer, or you could be like me and it could take a while to build up to it! Either way, God will instruct you in how to fast and God isn't going to be super angry with you if you mess up. GRACE!! Just keep practicing and practicing until it becomes a lifestyle for you. The more you do it, the easier it will become.

58

Say Hi!

> *Don't withhold good from someone who deserves it, when it is in your power to do so. Proverbs 3:27*
>
> *Generous persons will prosper; those who refresh others will themselves be refreshed. Proverbs 11:25*

Have you ever had someone cross your mind and then they end up reaching out to you or you end up seeing them in person soon after thinking of them? I believe most of us (probably all of us) have experienced this. This is God's way of telling you to reach out to this person or to pray for this person! Do not dismiss the thoughts of others! If you have an inclination to reach out and call/text someone you haven't spoken to in a while, follow through with it! You never know what the other person could be experiencing. God could have put this person on your heart because he wants you to encourage them and pray for them, or he may put this person on your heart because he wants to use them to encourage you! Don't shy away from saying hi! It can be so easy for us to get caught up in the day-to-day motions that we forget to reach out to others or we procrastinate in doing so! Try your best not to do that because each day is precious and you might be stealing a blessing from that individual or from yourself! So, just say hi!!!

59

Speak to the Wind

> *Then he said to me, "Prophesy to the breath; prophesy, son of man, and say to it, "This is what the Sovereign Lord says: Come, breath, from the four winds and breathe into these slain, that they may live." Ezekiel 37:9*

In Genesis, God tells Adam that he has given him dominion over all things in the world. When you have the holy spirit inside of you and you are a child of God, you are given authority! This authority and dominion mean that you can speak a thing and see it manifest if it is in God's will for your life and if it lines up with his promises for you! If you see things in your life that are not lining up with God's word, prophesy to them and tell them to come into alignment with the word of God!

It is absolutely crucial that we are always speaking out the word of God over our lives because the enemy comes to kill, steal, and destroy! And the weapon that the Lord gave us is his living and breathing word. We can speak it out and watch mountains move!!! Do not grow weary in doing good! Keep speaking truth over your situation no matter what it looks like. Satan will do everything in his power to try and deceive you. As soon as you hear or see a lie- speak to it!! Do not remain quiet! Just like Ezekiel speaks to the dry bones and prophesies to the four winds, do the same!!! Tell those things that are dead in your life, to come alive in Jesus' name!

60

⟨⟨≋⟩⟩

The Road to Consistency

> *For the moment, all discipline seems painful rather than pleasant, but later it yields the peaceful fruit of righteousness to those who have been trained by it. Hebrews 12:11*

Discipline and consistency, I believe, are two of the most important things that we can grow in as human beings! Growing in our walk with Christ requires these two skills. God's word says that when we seek him and his kingdom, all other things will be added to us! I believe, that if you can build a disciplined and consistent lifestyle of seeking God and growing your relationship with him, he will teach you how and where to place discipline and consistency in all other areas of your life. When you can learn to commit to forming a habit in your life of spending time with God, you will also learn how to form other positive habits in your life. This can range from business, health, personal relationships, etc.

You must learn consistency in order to increase your effectiveness and your quality of life! The road to consistency and discipline, is a bumpy one! It is supposed to be! You are human. You are not a robot. You are going to mess up. A lot. Trust me. That is good! You want to mess up because that means that you are trying! The key to building your ability to be consistent and disciplined is that when you mess up, get back on the train and try again! It also helps to have an accountability partner. I want to encourage you, if you are not already doing this, to find a specific free time in your day that you are going to devote to the Lord. This means a time where you are going to grab your bible, pray, read, and sit and listen to what the holy spirit wants to say and JOURNAL! It may take you a while to make this a daily habit in your life; it took a few years of practice for me until it became something that was a part of my every day routine! I spent many of the first few years falling off the train and forgetting to get back on for a period of time, and also many occasions of falling asleep while praying and reading. But I never fall asleep during my time with God anymore! You will grow in this if you haven't already! Once you form this habit in your life, it will be so much easier to build discipline and consistency in the other areas of your life! If you learn how to do it in one area, (and what better area to start in, than with your relationship with God), you can learn how to do it in all other areas of your life!!

61

◈

Throw Away Your Expectations

> *Fear not, for I am with you; be not dismayed, for I am your God; I will strengthen you, I will help you, I will uphold you with my righteous right hand. Isaiah 41:10*

We as humans can be really needy sometimes. We can start to lean on people too much and expect more out of people than we should. Have you ever found yourself expecting someone to be there for you and then when you needed them the most, they weren't there? I'm sure you have! I can pretty much guarantee every single one of us has endured that painful feeling. It's the worst. Especially when it is someone that means the world to us.

Here is something that pain and God's wisdom has taught me: I have to throw away my expectations of others. I no longer expect someone to be there for me if I am struggling and I also don't expect their support. Do I hope for it? Of course! But I do not need it! This requires a mindset shift. This requires you to learn how to look towards God for absolutely every single area of your life. If you have a problem, go to God first! If someone hurt you, go to God and forgive that person and let God kiss your wounds! Wounds from lovers, lack of support, or hurtful words cannot touch the outpouring of God's love in your life. This does not mean to forsake community or to build walls!!! Please do not do that. Please also share your heart with those that you can trust; but just always go to God first.

The point is, humans are prone to let you down, we are imperfect! It's just how it goes! When you can learn to turn to God in all ways of your life, life will become so much easier and happier for you!

62

⚜

Press On

*I press on toward the goal for the prize
of the upward call of God in Christ Jesus.
Philippians 3:14*

When you are being pressed on every side, it can feel seemingly impossible to continue to press on. Whatever struggle you may be facing right now, it's no match for King Jesus. Remember, the holy spirit resides in you. There is no mountain too big and there is no giant too strong that you cannot defeat through the power of Jesus. God is calling you to press on, always! Press on, unto the mark! You will finish the race that he has set before you. Maybe you're reading this and thinking, this is a lot easier said than done. Maybe you're thinking that you hear what I am saying, but you have no idea what "pressing on" actually looks like for you. Whatever is going through your mind right now, I am here to tell you that pressing on for you means to trust in Jesus and keep taking steps forward. You may have no idea what you are even supposed to be stepping towards- but that's what faith is! Faith is walking in the dark and trusting that God is holding your hand. He is a good father! He will not let you fall. Ask God for his help to continue to press on! He will get you through any and every battle in your life.

63

What is the Meaning of Life?

> *For we are God's handiwork, created in Christ Jesus to do good works, which God prepared in advance for us to do. Ephesians 2:10*

It is a common occurrence for people to question their reasoning for being alive at least once in their lifetime. So why is it that you are alive and breathing? Why did you grow up in the city that you did? Why did you have the parents or the lack thereof that you did? Is your life meaningful or meaningless? To sum up the answer to all of these resounding "why's": you were created with purpose. Yes, you! The plate you were given, was chosen by God. The adversity you faced, was used to build your character. If you have breath in your lungs, there is a reason for you walking on this earth.

God had a plan for you before you were even in your mother's womb! He had already written out every day of your life. Maybe you already know some of what God's plans for you are or maybe you are clueless. Either way, I ask that you ask the Lord to reveal more of his purpose for you today. Ask God to show you more of who you are in him. Your life is meaningful, not meaningless. Your life is meant to be a testimony to the power of Jesus. Your life is meant to be a blessing to others.

Ask yourself if you have been walking with God and if you have been in alignment with his perfect will for your life. If not, the evidence will be there. Anything outside of God's will is miserable. If you have been living in misery, ask God to set your heart on fire for him. Ask him to guide you in spending time with him so that you can fall in love with him, and then fall in love with the process and the purpose that he has for your life. There is more meaning to your life than you realize!

64

Course Correction

> *I know that you can do all things; no purpose of yours can be thwarted. Job 42:2*

Keep your eyes on Jesus and he will show you the way! Any time you are faced with making tough decisions, put it in the hands of God and wait for his direction and instruction. There is no need for you to worry or to stress about missing the mark! If you accidentally make a wrong turn, God will be quick to correct your course! God will walk this out with you and hold your hand the entire way- not just in the big things, but in the small things in your life as well! You will get to your destination! You may feel like you're lost sometimes, but trust that the creator of the map will get you to where you are supposed to be! Not only will he get you to your destination, but he will get you there right on time!

65

Count The Cost

> *For which of you, desiring to build a tower, does not first sit down and count the cost, whether he has enough to complete it? Luke 14:28*

It cost to live like this! The life of serving God will involve many sacrifices but there will always be a greater return! The question is, will you go when God calls you to go somewhere? Will you leave behind the familiar for the unknown? The cost of this life is exactly that: YOUR life! Are you willing to lay down your life to pick up the cross of Jesus before you and follow HIS plans for your life? This is your sweet reminder today that the price of walking with Jesus is giving up your own life in order to receive the greater life that God has planned for you. Will there be ups and downs? Of course! Will the sacrifices be hard to make at times? Yes! But it will always be worth it! Because paying this price, is an investment! It only yields greater returns! Greater returns of joy, peace, and fulfillment!

66

⁂

Silence the Voice of Doubt

If any of you lacks wisdom, let him ask God, who gives generously to all without reproach, and it will be given him. But let him ask in faith, with no doubting, for the one who doubts is like a wave of the sea that is driven and tossed by the wind. For that person must not suppose that he will receive anything from the Lord; he is a double-minded man, unstable in all his ways. James 1:5-8

There are many promises the Lord has made to me that I have not seen come to pass yet. Just because I haven't seen them yet, does not change what God has said he will do in my life! The same goes for you, just because you haven't seen the manifestation of God's promises, does not mean that they won't come to pass. Because they will! Due to waiting on these promises, my faith in some areas recently was starting to waver a bit. The voice of doubt began to infiltrate my mind. Once this began happening, the Lord took me to various scriptures and began rebuking me for the doubt. I wasn't going around speaking my doubts out loud, but it was still inside of my mind and heart... and God heard it!

If your heart has the slightest bit of doubt in it, God sees it and he will call it out to you. The Lord sent me specifically to James 1:5-8. This scripture shook me! Yes, I had read it before, but sometimes verses will hit a lot harder when you're in the middle of it or when God is disciplining you!

Stand in your faith! Do not waver! Silence the voice of doubt. If it arises in your mind, rebuke the spirit of doubt aloud. If you don't know how to do that, all that means is to say "I rebuke any spirit of doubt within me and cancel all lies of the enemy. I am walking by faith, not by my sight! I believe your promises are true, Lord".

One good reason you may not be seeing the manifestation of some things in your life, could be because you do not have the faith to receive it! Change the script in your mind from doubt to faith and watch God move on your behalf!

67

Faith Killers

> The light shines in the darkness, and the darkness did not comprehend it. John 1:5
>
> But a natural man does not accept the things of the Spirit of God, for they are foolishness to him; and he cannot understand them, because they are spiritually appraised. 1 Corinthians 2:14

Oh boy! This world has far too many faith killers walking around on these streets! A faith killer is someone that you share information with, for example- sharing God's plans for your life, and they automatically shoot it down with negativity. Faith killers do not believe in greatness. They lack the ability to stretch their mind to see how powerful God can work through individuals. Faith killers are like those that heard Noah was building an arc and they thought he was absolutely insane. Faith killers walk by sight, not by faith.

God has taught me to be very mindful and wise about who I share information with. Not everyone has the same faith that you do! If God tells you to stay quiet about something, you better heed to that! It is always for a good reason. There are far too many people that do not want to see you win. And there are far too many people that do not carry great faith. They will never understand you.

If you are fire, "faith killers" are the water! As soon as you open up to them, they throw water on you and will put your fire out! Faith killers will plant seeds of doubt into your mind and cause you to second guess if you heard God correctly. Always ask God for permission to share what he has shown you or to share what you are currently working on. Not everyone has to know what is happening in your life! It is better to work in silence and let your work speak for itself.

People may be against you, but God never is. Ask the Lord today to help you use your wisdom when speaking with others. Ask God to protect you from those that are faith killers and to surround you with like-minded individuals. Never give room for anyone to try and put out your fire! Fan those flames!

68

Shine Bright

> *No one lights a lamp and then puts it under a basket. Instead, a lamp is placed on a stand, where it gives light to everyone in the house. Matthew 5:15*

God's desire for our lives is that we walk fully in the spirit. God doesn't want to see us tango between the world and the spirit. Some people think serving and worshipping God is only for Sunday's or only when you're at some type of church function. Serving and worshipping God should be a part of your everyday life! God's word says that no one puts a light under a basket, but they put the light on the lampstand for everyone to see! You are a light for God! You need to be shining for him everywhere you go. Do not hide your light from the world to see. People shouldn't have to guess if you are

Christian. You should walk so boldly that it isn't a secret! Ask the Lord to give you courage to be a light everywhere that you go. Tell the Lord that you want to be a pleasing aroma to him. Tell him that you want your heart to be so on fire for him that it is obvious that you are his child to everyone that you meet!

69

Don't be a Chatty Kathy

> *Do not let any unwholesome talk come out of your mouths, but only what is helpful for building others up according to their needs, that it may benefit those who listen. Ephesians 4:29*

I remember when I was little, my nana (who raised me) was telling me about her dad and how he was such a man of God and very well respected! She told me that one of his greatest qualities was that you would never hear him speak badly about anyone! If he heard people gossiping, he would walk away. I have no idea why that story stuck with me the way that it did, but I am glad that it did. When she told me that, I decided that I was going to be the same way! I've always been very proud that I could carry myself in that manner and not join in in the bad mouthing of others. I'm sure I've gossiped before, but it's never been something that was an issue for me or a reoccurring sin!

People that choose to not engage in conversations that involve speaking poorly of others are highly respected and honorable individuals. God is so proud of his children when he sees them keeping their mouth shut and not gossiping!

Talking too much can often get us in trouble! I understand that gossiping can be a hard thing to quit! Especially when you're surrounded by a group of friends whose conversation revolves around the "talk of the town." Be the person who stands up in these conversations and says "Yeah, I'm not going to speak on that because who knows the actual truth concerning the story! That's their business." Or just walk away from the group and find other people to chat with.

If you struggle with gossiping, ask the Lord to help you to be slow to speak! Ask God to give you the boldness to speak up and defend others who aren't there to defend themselves!

70

Catch Those Judgmental Thoughts!

> *Do not judge, or you too will be judged. For in the same way you judge others, you will be judged, and with the measure you use, it will be measured to you. "Why do you look at the speck of sawdust in your brother's eye and pay no attention to the plank in your own eye?" Matthew 7:1-3*

You could be the nicest person in the world and still have a judgmental thought come into your brain! Bam! They can come out of nowhere sometimes!

But it's what you do with that thought that matters. If you allow your brain to entertain those judging thoughts, you will speak those judgments out loud and will end up hurting others. As Christians, we should embody love like Jesus. Learning to capture any judgmental thought, repenting, and giving it to Jesus is the best method to follow! Our brain can get so carried away if we let it! I know we've talked about this a few times in this devotional, but truly, be mindful of what you are thinking of and for how long you let those thoughts start to unravel in your brain. If you allow a seed of judgment to be planted in your brain, it will grow! And we don't want to sow any bad seeds!

Ask the Lord to teach you how to see people by their heart and how to love them and accept them even in their weaknesses.

7I

Offence is a Fence

> *A brother offended is more unyielding than a strong city, and quarreling is like the bars of a castle. Proverbs 18:19*

"Offence is a fence" is a quote I've heard a few times! I'm uncertain who the quote originates from. When we hold grievances towards others and allow offence to take its place, we build fences around ourselves that do not allow anyone in. It can be very difficult to deal with people who are easily offended because you are constantly having to walk on egg-shells with them to be careful not to set them off. The spirit of offence sucks! It will literally suck the life out of you and others.

If you find yourself getting offended easily, this means you must get to the root of the issue. Ask the Lord to help you identify what all of your triggers are. Then proceed to ask the Lord where all of this started. Memories will begin to surface and when they do, this is when you forgive the offender, forgive yourself, and ask the Lord to heal these wounds. Offence is so heavy, let it go!

7²

What If?

You keep him in perfect peace whose mind is stayed on you, because he trusts in you. Isaiah 26:3

Today, let's make an agreement to throw the question "what if?" in the trash! We are making strides to walk in bold kingdom faith! We do not have room to begin playing the game "If I do this, what if this happens." The moral of the story is "If you obey God, blessings will happen!" There is no questioning God. If you have given him your heart, he is going to make certain that all things will work together for your good! We don't have time to let our thoughts run amok and cause us unnecessary stress! What a waste of time! God's word says that he knows the exact number of hairs on our head! If he cares about something so tiny, don't you think he cares enough to make sure that you are not led astray! Drop the worries today! We ain't got time for that, kingdom kid!!!

73

Bending Over Backwards

> *But those who wait on the Lord shall renew their strength. They shall mount up with wings like eagles, they shall run and not be weary, they shall walk and not faint.*
> *Isaiah 40:31*

Keep doing good! I know that you may catch yourself bending over backwards for people and receiving nothing in return. I know it's hard to feel invisible or unappreciated, but God is seeing every act of goodness that you have poured into this world. God sees you! Do not forget that. Not only is he preparing rewards for you in heaven, but he is also preparing rewards for you on earth! God will not let your works go unrewarded!

God is going to bless your harvest with an abundance

and overflow of his goodness and blessings! Rise up from the grave of feeling sorry for yourself. You are ultimately loved by the creator of this Earth. Keep up the good work! You are doing amazing. God loves a cheerful heart, so let every act of goodness that you do, be done with thanksgiving! Do not expect anything in return when you are helping others, do it out of the goodness of your heart and know that God will be certain to reward you!!!

74

Chasing Diamonds

> *Do not lay up for yourselves treasures on earth, where moth and rust destroy and where thieves break in and steal, but lay up for yourselves treasures in heaven, where neither moth nor rust destroys and where thieves do not break in and steal. For where your treasure is, there your heart will be also. Matthew 6:19-21*

Put away the foolish things of this world and fix your eyes on Jesus. I know the desire can burn so strongly in us to want to do well for ourselves, make a name for ourselves, and live a life of financial prosperity. But we must keep our heart in check! What is your ultimate desire? Is it to chase after the things of this world? Or to chase after Jesus? We have to constantly ask the Lord to seek our heart to reveal if there is any wrong way in us. Chasing after diamonds will leave you striving and always hungry for more. But chasing after Jesus will keep you at peace and fully satisfied! The world will never offer you what Jesus can.

75

Develop In Me A Willing Spirit

I do not understand what I do. For what I want to do I do not do, but what I hate I do. And if I do what I do not want to do, I agree that the law is good. As it is, it is no longer I myself who do it, but it is sin living in me. For I know that good itself does not dwell in me, that is, in my sinful nature. For I have the desire to do what is good, but I cannot carry it out. For I do not do the good I want to do, but the evil I do not want to do- this I keep on doing. Now if I do what I do not want to do, it is no longer I who do it, but it is sin living in me that does it. Romans 7:15-20

Battling with the flesh and spirit is torturous. I used to struggle majorly with committing sins that I knew I didn't need to partake in. My heart did not want to commit them but I still did them anyways! In my past, I related heavily with today's scripture. It was the love of Jesus that brought me out of the cycle of heavy battle with flesh and spirit. The love of Jesus pulled me in close and gave me a heart that desired more of his presence. Jesus' love is what set me free and broke off the bondage in my life. His loving kindness is what pulled on my heart and gave me a deep desire to please him and obey him. I encountered his love through spending time with Him and reading His word. Meditate on the word of God and ask the Lord to develop in you a willing spirit! A spirit that desires to obey Him and do his will!

76

Harsh Reality

> *Do not be deceived: God is not mocked, for whatever one sows, that will he also reap. For the one who sows to his own flesh will from the flesh reap corruption, but the one who sows to the Spirit will from the Spirit reap eternal life. Galatians 6:7-8*
>
> *If we confess our sins, he is faithful and righteous to forgive us our sins and to cleanse us from all unrighteousness. 1 John 1:9*

Have you ever stood in the middle of a mess and asked God, "Why me?! Why did you allow this to happen" and then realize that you were the one that made the mess? Every action we take has a consequence. If we choose to sin and walk outside of God's perfect will for us, there will always be consequences for our actions. We cannot look up at God and blame him for our mistakes. The Lord made certain to give you his word and warn you of the consequences of sin. God doesn't give us these instructions because he wants to keep you away from pleasure, but because he wants to protect you. True pleasure comes from pleasing and obeying God, not from the things of this world. If you are standing in a mess right now and you are mad at God, take a step back, and see if you were the one to light the fire to the match.

What's amazing is, if you made a mess for yourself, and you repent- God will clean up the mess you made! He is such a good father to forgive us when we sin and have asked for his forgiveness. Will you still experience consequences for your sin, yes! But will God restore all that's broken when you go to him and repent, yes!

77

Victim or Victor?

> *And we know that in all things God works for the good of those who love him, who have been called according to his purpose. Romans 8:28*

Life doesn't happen to you, it happens for you! I love that quote! Life is so sweet when you live with the victor mentality rather than the victim mentality. Do you find yourself blaming all of your problems on other people and past experiences? If the answer is yes, there is hope! Switching from a victim to victor mindset requires awareness and mindfulness on how you perceive life's experiences. When Joseph's brothers sold him into slavery and he ended up in prison, he continued to praise God. Out of his adversity, God birthed promises and sent Joseph to the palace. That adversity happened for him, not to him! If Joseph lived his life as a victim, his mind would be focused on plotting evil towards his brothers while in prison. His mind would have been focused on "Woe is me. There is no light at the end of this tunnel. I might as well rot here and die." That type of victim mindset does not give room for the victor mindset! Joseph would not have seen God's promises for him if he would've lived as a victim and would have given up and focused on his misery and all of those that wronged him. But praise God, Joseph did not choose to think that way! Joseph was a victor, and so are you! We are kingdom citizens, victory runs in our blood because of Jesus! We must live with the victory mindset. If you struggle with having a victim mentality, ask the Lord today to heal you from past wounds, forgive the people that hurt you, and praise God for outcomes that you haven't even seen yet! Praise God today for his goodness and faithfulness because he works ALL things together for the good for those that love Him!

78

He is Worthy To Be Praised

> *But seek first the kingdom of God and his righteousness, and all these things will be added to you. Matthew 6:33*

Whether we have seen God's hand move in our situation or not, God is worthy to be praised! Our hearts desire should be for more of him and his presence- this should be first and foremost. We should all make it a constant habit to do a heart check and see if we are seeking more of the HAND of God, rather than seeking the FACE of God. Are we seeking the presence of God or the presents of God?

When waiting to see God move, it can be easy for our hearts to slip into a place of constantly seeking the gifts of

God. The more you mature in the things of God, the more you will learn to posture your heart in a place of constantly just seeking his FACE. We already have everything we need. If we look with our physical eyes, we may not see that God has already made a way and provided for us. But if we cling to the word of God and we see with the eyes of the spirit, we will know "what more could we have need of?! We have the holy spirit living inside of us, a personal relationship with God, and eternity waiting for us in the Kingdom of God." God's word is true and never changes. We can stand on that. Let's have hearts that have faith in all that he has promised us and begin to walk in already knowing we have everything we need. When we do this, we make room for the face of God in our lives. We make room for deeper, closer, and more personal relationship with the father above. Worship your father today! Sing to Him. Thank him for WHO He is. He is so worthy to be praised.

79

"Vengeance is Mine"

> *Do not take revenge, my dear friends, but leave room for God's wrath, for it is written: "It is mine to avenge; I will repay," says the Lord. Romans 11:29*

I'm telling you! When someone does us dirty, our flesh is ready to retaliate! Whether you go for more of a brunt action and you're showing up ready to throw hands or you go for a "softer" approach and plan to give them the cold shoulder...the flesh is sinful and will try to plant seeds of retaliation if you allow it to. The more you walk in step with the father, the more you will die to the sinful nature of your flesh. God's word instructs us to do good to those that harm us! Definitely not something the world preaches. But Jesus does! God promises us, that vengeance is his. God is a just

God. He will be certain that all things are weighed with righteous judgement. When you bless those that hurt you, God will bless you. People call it karma when they sit back and watch life throw at them, what they have thrown at others. But it isn't karma my dear friend, it is our sovereign God in heaven being certain that the scales of judgment are balanced in righteousness.

Do you struggle with biting your tongue, plotting evil for evil, or being ready to throw hands? If so, ask the Lord to give you a heart that desires to please him. Ask God today to help you lay all of your problems into his hands and allow him to avenge you. Learn to start forgiving and praying for your enemies and God will change your heart. All of your problems, are in his hands!

80

Create in Me A Clean Heart

> *Create in me a clean heart, O God; and renew a right spirit within me. Psalm 51:10*

Do you ever sit back and think about how far God has brought you and just be in awe at the strides you've made partnering with the Lord? On the flip side of this, do you ever come face to face with a circumstance that rises old behaviors to the surface, and you may respond in a not so Christian-like manner? Then you just sit back and you're like, "dang, I didn't realize that was still hiding in me! I thought I was a little holier than this..."

It's so interesting to see the deep works that God continues to do in our lives, and yet also see some residue from our past still try to attach itself to our inner being.

One area that I believe we may all struggle in, is our mouth! Losing our temper, outbursts of anger, getting snippy with people, needing to get the last word in, etc. From my own experience, my struggle with my mouth lately has been with my beautiful daughter during homework time! That second-grade homework and common core mess is something else! I have had countless experiences of losing my temper during homework and then when all is said and done, I feel so horrible. I apologize to my daughter and explain that those were not appropriate ways for me to respond and that I am working on being better and slower to speak.

Can you relate with me when it comes to having a problem with your mouth? What the Lord revealed to me was, as I continue to pray for the Lord to create a clean heart in me, my words and reactions will be made purer. Because, "Out of the mouth, flow the issues of the heart!"

If you are struggling with your temper and your responses to frustration, pray Psalm 51 over yourself daily. Ask God to create a clean heart in you. Keep sitting at the feet of Jesus so he can clean out the clutter in your heart and make you slow to speak, slow to anger, and abounding in love.

81

Good Shepherd

> *What do you think? If someone had one hundred sheep and one of them wandered off, wouldn't he leave the ninety-nine on the hillside and go and search for the stray? Matthew 18:12*

If you were unaware, sheep are known to have no sense of direction and they aren't seen as the most intelligent species. If a herd of sheep are without a shepherd, they are lost!

That is just like us! If we are without the great Shepherd, Yahweh, we are absolutely clueless. A life without God is a life uncertain of direction. A life without the good, good shepherd, leads straight to death and destruction.

I read a story prior to writing this about a group of 400 sheep walking straight off a cliff into their doom because their shepherd decided to go eat some breakfast. Wow! Imagine if God said, "Hey, I think I will take today off from being God/from being your shepherd." If he did, the whole world would be in greater chaos than it already is.

Praise God, he never leaves us and is our shepherd always! He never fails to guide us. But for some reason, us as his sheep, sometimes have tendencies to wander off from him. It's not God that decides to stop shepherding us, but it is US that sometimes choose to stop being his sheep!

But just like a good shepherd, when we are his, even when we wander off, God will leave the 99 sheep just to find the one that wandered off!

Take some time today after reading this devotion to just praise God for the good shepherd that he is and will always be!!!

82

⚜

Communication Error

> *But the wisdom from above is first pure,*
> *then peaceable, gentle, open to reason,*
> *full of mercy and good fruits, impartial and*
> *sincere. James 3:17*

God gifted us with the gift of relationship with others. Relationships are such a blessing and beautiful thing to have. But with relationships, can come friction! Instead of viewing this friction as a negative thing, let's begin to view it as an opportunity for growth between both parties!

There are always ups and downs within every relationship, but we should never allow the downs to last longer than a moment!

There are so many working parts to a relationship that it can be very easy for two different people, from different backgrounds, and different histories to run into communication problems!

But how is it that we should best handle these communication errors?

It takes much growth and wisdom from God to learn how to handle communication errors appropriately and effectively.

Misunderstandings can cause people to hold grudges for eternity! But that is not how God calls us to respond to these situations.

We must learn to be open to understanding where others are coming from. We must take the time to do introspection on ourselves to see if we are hearing and seeing things through the lens of trauma. It is so important for us to bring our misunderstandings and errors of communication to the Lord and allow him to deal with it.

Let it go and give it to God.

Ask God today to help you better navigate future misunderstandings and miscommunications that happen in your relationships. Ask the Lord for increased wisdom and patience in your relationships. You will grow in the area of communication!

83

Partnering With God

> *So the last shall be first, and the first last: for many be called, but few chosen. Matthew 20:16*

Life is a wild ride, but it is even wilder when you make the decision to partner with God. A lot of times, partnering with God can look like you are going backwards initially. But over the past couple of years, God has taught me that when I am walking in faith with him, and it looks like I'm going nowhere, he actually has me in his slingshot.

With your obedience, there will be times in your life where God has you in his slingshot and he pulls you so far back, only to launch you into your full purpose and calling! So initially, when you say yes, things may be going no where or seem to have no momentum at all. In all actuality, God just has you in a still, quiet place for preparation. But, get ready, because when he lets go of you in the slingshot, you are going to be launched at full speed!

84

The Friend of God

> *I no longer call you servants because a servant does not know his master's business. Instead, I have called you friends, for everything that I learned from my father I have made known to you. John 15:15*

A couple of weeks ago, I was crying out to God and praising him and I said "Lord, you are my best friend. I pray that you see me as your friend too." Soon after that, the sweet father had me open up my bible directly to what today's scripture is.

Crocodile tears, okay!

There are seasons in life that we all go through, where it can feel pretty lonely! There are times where it feels like you don't have the support that you crave from your friends and family. Often times, you may feel misunderstood.

I want to encourage you today by reminding you that you have a friend in Jesus. And if you choose to be his servant, even better, he calls YOU his friend.

God holds so many titles in our lives, and with him being so sovereign, how neat and loving is it to know that the King of all Kings, calls you friend!

You should be wearing a huge smile for the rest of your day/night (depending on when you're reading this) knowing that the Lord is your friend!

He will always be there for you and he knows you better than anyone else ever will. The only perfect friend there is.

85

Exercise It!

> *He gives strength to the weary and increases the power of the weak. Isaiah 40:29*
>
> *But as for you, be strong and do not give up, for your work will be rewarded. 2 Chronicles 15:7*

You know when you exercise and lift heavier than normal or when you do a new activity that your body is not used to? Afterwards, you can tend to be pretty sore! It can be tricky to sit down and difficult to walk at times when you are sore.

So what do we all do when we have sore muscles? We stretch!

A couple of months ago I was in the gym stretching out my sore muscles, trying to work the kinks out! In the middle of doing this, the Lord gives me revelation. This was it:

There will be times in your life where God calls you out of the old, into something new. A new position or to move to a new place. When you follow through with the new he is giving you, it often feels super heavy and uncomfortable! It's hard to walk in the new because it's so unfamiliar.

You're carrying something new so it works new "muscles" of your mind!

All those "muscles" need, are some stretching!

Are you following me?

What I mean is, keep exercising/stretching in the new place/position the Lord has you in, and it will work out the knots and kinks on it's own! It will become more comfortable and you will be able to walk in this new thing with more ease and more strength!

86

Be Plugged In

> *And let us not neglect our meeting together, as some people do, but encourage one another, especially now that the day of his return is drawing near. Hebrews 10:25*
>
> *For where two or three are gathered in my name, I am there in the midst of them. Matthew 18:20*
>
> *For just as we have many members in one body and all the members do not have the same function, so we, who are many, are one body in Christ, and individually members one of another. Romans 12:4-5*

There is something about the power of the body of Christ when two or three or more are gathered in Jesus name! Each of us bring something different to the table. Maybe you're an arm and your neighbor is a leg, then you join with the rest of the believers, and you have a whole body!

Each part of the body plays it's own role but they all work together to form a functioning, powerful, body!

It is so important to be plugged into the right church family. I felt the Lord call me out of my old church because he was wanting to take me somewhere new. But then, I was out of church for almost two years. I continued to spend daily time with God and let him constantly minister to me and teach me. But, something was missing! I craved a church that was fit for me and what I needed.

Community, I cannot stress enough, is so important.

The enemy targets unity, always. He targets marriages and any where that two or more believers are joined. HE knows the power that two or more believers carry together!

We should also be just as aware how powerful we are in unity for Christ!

If you are not plugged in anywhere, ask the Lord today to direct you to the perfect church that is most fitting for you. Follow his promptings. He will send you to a new place!

Not too long ago, I prayed and asked the Lord for a church that would be perfect for me to plug into, and the next day, someone messaged me on Facebook inviting me to their church out of the blue. And I haven't stopped going since. It was perfect for me and exactly what I was missing!

I want you to know, you will be so unbelievably blessed when you plug in.

And for those of you that do have a home church, you know exactly what I am talking about! So I just want to continue to encourage you to remember how important it is to stay connected to the body! And to remind you of the power the church has when it is unified as one!

87

Church Hurt

> *We must keep our eyes on Jesus, who leads us and makes our faith complete. He endured the shame of being nailed to a cross, because he knew that later on he would be glad he did. Now he is seated at the right side of God's throne! So keep your mind on Jesus, who put up with many insults from sinners. Then you won't get discouraged and give up. Hebrews 12:2-4*

My heart literally breaks when I hear stories of individuals that no longer will step foot inside of a church because of the trauma that they experienced there. I can't even imagine the fire that burns in the Lord's heart when he see's his children treated poorly. If you have experienced this, I want to tell you personally that I am so sorry that you ever had to receive poor treatment. I want to let you know that just because you experienced this, this doesn't mean that all church bodies function the same way. And it is NOT, how they should function, period. But the Lord will have his way with those that have caused people to turn away from the Lord.

I want to encourage you and tell you that there is a church place for you to step foot inside and serve the Lord, as well as build a group of friendships that you can do life with. A place that feels like home!

I justified for a while my reasons for not attending church, but like I said yesterday, once I finally got plugged back in... I was missing a piece of my life that I didn't even realize how bad I needed until I walked in and was surrounded by love.

May we all remember that we cannot always look to people to exemplify who God is and what relationship with God looks like. Because unfortunately, there are people that are wolves in sheep's clothing. There are also people that claim Jesus, yet they have no personal relationship with the father and their fruits expose who they are. And also, don't forget that we're human and prone to sin. Therefore, we can't expect to be surrounded by humans and never get hurt!

May we all strive to seek Jesus with every inch of our being so he transforms us and we can be the LOVE that the world needs. May we be the people that welcome ALL and not judge books by their cover. May we all be a little more like Jesus each and every day. Church hurt shouldn't even be a thing, but with it existing, let's all join together to make a difference in the body and be the example that we are called to be! Keep your eyes on Jesus!!!

88

Dig Up Those Talents!

He also who had received the one talent came forward, saying, "Master, I knew you to be a hard man, reaping where you did not sow, and gathering where you scattered no seed, so I was afraid, and I went and hid your talent in the ground. Here, you have what is yours." But his master answered him, "You wicked and slothful servant! You knew that I reap where I have not sown and gather where I scattered no seed? Then you ought to have invested my money with the bankers, and at my coming I should have received what was my own with interest. So take the talent from him and give it to him who has the ten talents. For to everyone who has will more be

> *given, and he will have an abundance. But from the one who has not, even what he has will be taken away. Matthew 25:24-29*

In the bible there is a story about a master and a few of his workers. To each worker he gives them a specific number of talents (a form of currency) according to their ability and tells them to go out and work with what they have. Two of the workers multiply their talents, and the third worker decides to bury his! The workers that multiplied their talents were given more from the master, the one who buried his talent received nothing!

Catch the word "talent" there! It's a form of currency, but I also believe it refers to our "TALENTS" as well.

The Lord has been speaking this story to me for the past couple of weeks really highlighting on some of the talents he gave me when I was younger that I ended up burying underground and not touching. He has been telling me to pick them up again!

Ask yourself if you had any talents as a child that you are not currently putting to use now? God gave you those talents for a reason and he wants you to put them to use so he can multiply them!

89

Liar, Liar Pants on Fire!

> *The thief comes only to steal and kill and destroy; I have come that they may have life, and have it to the full. John 10:10*

Ugh! Satan is the biggest liar that ever existed. Listen, and I need you to listen clearly. The LAST thing Satan wants to see you doing is to see you walking in the fullness of what God has called you to do! He will do everything in his power to make you doubt your God given abilities and talents.

Speaking of yesterday's devotion about burying talents... Satan will dig the hole for you and he waits for you to put it inside....and with each lie he feeds you, you end up throwing another shovel of dirt on top of that God given talent until you've walked away and completely forgotten all about it!

But guess what friends and family?! Today is the day that

we grab our shovel and uncover what Satan coerced us into burying! These talents of ours are coming back to life today!!!!

Do not skip this part!!! I need you to take the next couple of days to think about things that you were naturally good at or enjoyed doing when you were younger. I also want you to think about what your dream job was as a little kid. Wrapped up in these thoughts, is one or a few of your God given talents.

When Satan sees how God wants to use us, he will attack that very skill/talent relentlessly, beginning from your childhood, all the way up until he makes you forget that you even had those talents!

He will use people to downgrade you and your abilities. He will feed your head with lies telling you that you aren't good at anything. He will make sure that your work and your abilities aren't seen and he will make you feel like you are always in the background and unimportant.

So here I am reminding you, that Satan is a liar, liar, LITERAL pants on fire!!!!

Go get quiet before the Lord and ask him to help you uncover the lies of the enemy regarding your talents. These are the areas that God wants to use you the most!

Satan is going to wish he never messed with you!!!

90

Mighty Mountain Mover

> *So he said to me, "This is the word of the Lord to Zerubbabel: "Not by might nor by power, but by my spirit," says the Lord almighty. Zechariah 4:6*

Our God is a mighty mountain mover! There is no mountain in your life that is too big for our God. Have no fear or doubt because if God says he is going to do a thing in your life, he WILL do it. His promises are yes and amen! All it takes is for God to speak a word and command the mountain to move. All it takes is the wind of his spirit to blow on your mountain and cause it to crumble!

Look at your life and see if there are any mountains standing in your way. Increase your faith today in order to see those mountains move at God's appointed time. You may not see it yet, but they will move. What's so cool about these mountains, is that we can tend to see them as blockages to our path, but in all reality, they are there to build our endurance as we walk around them time and time again. Because, once God blows your mountains away, you will have such a renewed strength that you will plunge forward!

So here is a sweet reminder for you today: it is not by might, or by power, but by the SPIRIT OF GOD, that these mountains will be removed. Praise God today for removing the mountains in your life!

91

Bride Of Christ

The kingdom of heaven is like a king who prepared a wedding banquet for his son. He sent his servants to those who had been invited to the banquet to tell them to come, but they refused to come. Then he sent some more servants and said, "Tell those who have been invited that I have prepared my dinner: My oxen and fattened cattle have been butchered, and everything is ready. Come to the wedding banquet." "But they paid no attention and went off- one to his field, another to his business. Matthew 22:2-5

I've not been married yet, but I can only imagine how much excitement and anticipation is built up as a man and woman are waiting on their expected wedding day. Just imagine, how much more excited the Lord and angels are about our heavenly wedding! Imagine the place and the feast that the Lord has prepared for his bride- the church- when he brings us to our forever home. Oh, what a beautiful day that will be!

Think about all of the preparation that comes with planning for a wedding here on earth. Earthly weddings are only temporary but our heavenly wedding is for eternity. If so much preparation and planning is involved with our earthly weddings, imagine how much more preparation and planning is needed for the heavenly wedding.

God's word says that he is waiting for a spotless bride without wrinkle. This means it is absolutely crucial that all of God's children are doing the work of his kingdom to aid in preparing the body of Christ for Christ return and for our kingdom wedding. We are the body so each of us have our own personal role to play. There is no role that is too small or too big. Each person plays their part!

Ask the Lord how you can aid in preparing his people for his return. It doesn't matter what kind of occupation you are in; God will show you ways to edify his church, and he will show you how to impact the lost souls around you and in your workplace.

I encourage you to go read the rest of Matthew 22. It is time to get very serious about our walks with God and serious in leading/planting seeds in those that are lost around us. There is still SO much work to be done before the marvelous wedding day!!!

92

Keys to The Kingdom

> *I will place on his shoulder the key to the house of David; what he opens no one can shut, and what he shuts no one can open. Isaiah 22:22*

I am writing this devotional on 2/22/22. This date feels so prophetic. The Lord has brought to many believer's minds the scripture, Isaiah 22:22, in relation to today's date. This scripture pertains to keys being released to the kingdom.

God releases specific keys to individuals. The keys the Lord is talking about in this scripture symbolize authority that is given to the believer to open the doors of heaven for others to see what true Kingdom living looks like.

One of the purposes of these keys is to unlock something in others! These keys help build the body of the church. For example, I believe the Lord has given me a key to unlock increased faith in others. This basically means the Lord has given me the ability to help aid others in their journey of increasing their faith to believe for greater and to believe in the big plans that the Lord has for them.

Ask God today if he has given you any keys in order to unlock something in others. Know that if you are willing to go on this wild journey with the Lord, and if you have faith, he will place keys into your hand that will really aid in building the kingdom!!!

93

The Freedom of Christ

Now the Lord is the spirit, and where the spirit of the Lord is, there is freedom.
2 Corinthians 3:17

I am so thankful for the freedom that Christ brings. God comes into our lives to demolish the old creation and then rebuilds us into the new creation he had in mind originally. When we are born into this world, we enter in as sinners. But praise God, by his grace, he saves us! God's plan for our lives is for us to walk in his love and his freedom. He wants to set us free so that we are no longer bound by the sin that so easily entangles us.

Every single one of us have character flaws, traumas, addictions, etc. God wants to give you freedom in all of those areas.

Sometimes we can tend to get in our own way of our freedom because we think that we can break free from these things on our own. But we cannot. It is impossible. There will always be something there that will continue to try and keep us in bondage.

BUT, when God steps in, one by one he will remove those chains.

I want to tell you that Satan desires that you live in your shame and guilt. He desires for every single time you mess up, that you would remain in your shame. He wants to feed your mind with lies about who you are. He will speak to you telling you that you are a failure, you are no good, and why do you even try to change?

But God comes to you in love. He comes and asks that you will just surrender it all to Him. He desires that you seek him more and more and more. He just asks that you will ask him for forgiveness and for help in all of these areas.

If you trust in him, and continue seeking him, HE WILL SET YOU FREE from all of these areas that have held you in bondage.

I speak freedom into your life today and I believe that you will soar again. There is a new freedom coming to you. In due time. Praise God today for defeating every single one of your battles.

94

A New Day Dawning

> *You have turned for me my mourning into dancing; You have put off my sackcloth and clothed me with gladness, to the end that my glory may sing praise to you and not be silent. O Lord my God, I will give thanks to you forever. Psalm 30:11-12*

I know you've been tired and weary from it all. But God is calling you into a new day. These hardships you have faced, have been there to thicken your armor. For when new battles come your way in the future, your new armor can withstand the heat. God has been building you into this warrior that can come face to face with adversity and can use the authority of God's word to put out all of the fires that stand in your way.

God is saying that there is a "New Day Dawning" for you.

Have patience, be still and know that HE is God.

He is preparing a new season for you. A place where you will forget the pain of your past.

He is turning your mourning into dancing.

He is turning your crying into laughter.

He is turning the ashes into beauty.

There is a new day dawning.

Perk up! Because things will take a sudden turn. Once you fix your eyes on Jesus, you will see life differently and you will see things begin to change before your eyes.

God is a good God and he is giving you better.

Just believe.

95

Receive The Good Gifts

> *Every good and perfect gift is from above, coming down from the Father of the heavenly lights, who does not change like shifting shadows. James 1:17*

I have noticed that there are people that are so riddled with shame and guilt, and they have fed into the enemies lies so much, that when they are presented with GOD opportunities, they shut them down. They believe they don't have the ability to step into these new opportunities. They think they don't deserve it Fear and insecurities get in the way of them receiving something beautiful from the Lord.

Currently, relationships are running through my head. For some of you reading this, God is trying to give you a God ordained relationship. This could be a friendship or a future spouse. But you have allowed walls to be built over time and there is a disbelief in your heart that is telling you that this is "too good to be true." But those are lies from the enemy.

God is trying to give you really good gifts, but you must receive them. You must speak back to the lies in your head and speak God's truth over your life.

Receive the good gifts from the father!

Whether it's a new relationship or a new opportunity that you feel is from God, ask the Lord to remove the fear and lies from the enemy, so you can receive this beautiful thing.

96

Get Back Up Again

> *For though a righteous man falls seven times, he will rise again, but the wicked stumble into calamity. Proverbs 24:16*

Have you sinned again? God is saying just get back up! Any time that you fall short, go directly back to your father. God will rebuke us first, and then directly after his rebuke he comes swooping in with such love, grace, and mercy. Do not stay stuck in your guilt.

Majority of the time I am a healthy eater and I see no wrong in enjoying a "fatty" meal every once in a while! But I've experienced some times in the past where I would eat one "bad" meal and then my thought process would turn to, "Hey, I already ate one "bad" thing so I might as well just gorge myself and finish the rest of the day with filling myself with "bad foods"." Now that right there, is such an unhealthy way to live! I feel that this is how many Christians may view sin. "Well, I already sinned once today, I might as well just finish doing this sin for the rest of the day/week/month..."

God wants to remove this mindset from you! As soon as you fall short, ask God for his forgiveness, and get back up!! Go directly to his heart and love for you, and it will surely lead you to repentance. Just keep going!

97

Juxtaposition

> *Finally, all of you, have unity of mind, sympathy, brotherly love, a tender heart, and a humble mind. 1 Peter 3:8*

This morning in my time with the Lord he says the word "juxaposition." And listen you guys, don't laugh at me, but I had to look up the definition of the word because I had no idea. The definition of juxtaposition is essentially where you take two things and place them side by side in order to highlight comparisons and contrasts.

This is when the Lord began showing me how he will put different relationships in our life that are God ordained and he will use them to highlight comparisons and contrasts between the two individuals. It is in these contrasts, where each parties learn to grow.

These stark contrasts can either be viewed as barriers that allow no further access to be gained in the relationship, or they can be viewed as climbing walls that allow each party to take one step at a time in order to come to a better understanding of one another's differences and still be able to walk side by side even in the contrasts.

I was doing some reading on the word "juxtaposition" and I came across this article that talks about how our relationship with God is a juxtaposition. Given that our relationship with the Lord is the highest form of covenant relationship there is, I think it gives such a great picture of how the differences can create such beauty. We are unholy, yet God is holy and he chose to form a relationship with us. We are unrighteous, yet God clothes us in righteousness.

May we see the grace God has on us, and may we learn to give grace to others in their differences, the way the Lord does for us.

Ask the Lord today for an increase of grace on those in your life. I know it can be hard to navigate relationships when there are such differences, but God will show you that there is beauty in it. Though we may have differences, we are one in Christ.

98

Be Like a Child

> *"But I will restore you to health, and heal your wounds," declares the Lord. Jeremiah 30:17*

Think back to your childhood. You were worry free! You didn't have a care in the world. You didn't realize the craziness that was going on around you in the world or in your home- you just lived life and enjoyed it.

Although, for some of you, your innocence may have been stolen from you at such a young age that maybe you can't relate to this feeling.

I know for me, I had addicts in my family, and I had no awareness of what was going on until I was about 8 or 9 years old, and then after that I was clued in to what was going on. If you dealt with extreme traumatic experiences, I am not sure how that would have affected you as a child. But I just want to say if you had to experience anything that stole your childhood from you, I am so sorry. God never intended for you to be hurt in the ways that you were.

What's amazing about the Lord, is that he is outside of time and space. Therefore, the Lord can go back to your childhood, and he can redeem the time. He can restore the little girl or little boy in you. He can give you that feeling of being child-like, as an adult! He can erase all past traumas and hurts and cause you to live "like a child" again.

What I mean by this is, he can restore all things that are broken and you can begin to live care-free; knowing that your Father in Heaven has taken care of everything for you. You can enjoy life no matter what curveballs are thrown at you because you have been healed and redeemed by him. You've tasted his goodness, and you know that it never runs dry.

Think back to what age you saw the ugliness of this world and think about how Satan can work through other people to harm you.

Take the time now, to ask God to go back to that place with you when you were first hurt and ask him to heal it now. Ask him to redeem the time. Ask Him to make all things new for you.

Believe! He can redeem your childhood even as an adult. Let's all walk together in child-like faith!

99

The Torch is Yours

> *Whatever you do, work at it with all your heart, as working for the Lord, not for human masters since you know that you will receive an inheritance from the Lord as a reward. It is the Lord Christ you are serving. Colossians 3:23-24*

Be the forerunner in your family! For generations and generations, there are things that some of your past relatives were supposed to accomplish, but they never did. Maybe they didn't have the faith. Or maybe this whole time, it was just ordained for you to be the one that carried the torch!

There are inheritances in heaven that are stored up for you because of your faith and obedience. Whatever call the Lord has made on your life, be sure to follow it with all of your heart. There is no greater pleasure than doing the works that God has prepared for you ahead of time to do. Please do not let doubt or fear or naysayers get in the way of what God has spoken to you. The enemy is going to send people your way to tell you that what you're desiring to do, "isn't possible." People will tell you that you're crazy. But the thing is, you are not here to please people. And when you die, those haters, they aren't going to be the one's that you are speaking with concerning the things you did and didn't do while you were on Earth.

You are going to one day be face to face with the King of Kings and he is going to ask you, "What did you do for my name? How did you serve my kingdom?"

How would you answer him now?

Are you wasting any of your potential currently?

Have you settled for comfortable, easy, and "normal"?

Ask yourself these questions. Evaluate your life.

Have you been on track with what the Lord has asked of you?

If so, amazing! I am so proud of you.

If not, praise God! Because, today, you have taken time to evaluate your limiting beliefs. And now you have a chance to ask the Lord to stretch your faith and beliefs. All it takes is for you to make the decision to say yes to God. When you do, you will get to run with the torch that will bless generations after you! Your obedience will yield such a harvest. And when you die, your father will be so proud of you.

Also, please do not think that what God is asking of you has to be this huge grandeur thing. Because it doesn't. Whatever God is asking of you, big or small, that is what you are to do! The things that are deemed as small can bear a domino effect of mega impact. Those "small things" can be just as effective as the "big calls" are for the kingdom!!!

100

Running With God

> *"For I know the plans I have for you,"*
> *declares the Lord, "plans to prosper you*
> *and not to harm you, plans to give you*
> *hope and a future." Jeremiah 29:11*

I pray that with each day of this devotional that you have read, that it has spoken to you deeply. I want to leave you with the encouragement and motivation, to run, run, run, run, run with God in ALL things that you do. Run the race. See it to completion. You have an almighty God that wars for you on your behalf. He is not going to leave your side. Every step of the way, he is going to be guiding, directing, encouraging, and loving you. You have everything at your disposal to be successful in the call that God has on your life.

Also, may this become your main goal: To enter into

heavens gates one day and hear "Well done, my good and faithful servant." A life without God is meaningless.

There is purpose all over you. As you run with God, he will uncover pieces over time. He will show you how he used the hardships to make you more like him. He will show you over time why things had to happen the way that they did. I know some things don't make sense right now, but soon they will. TRUST.

He has such amazing plans for you, so whatever you do, do not stop running!!!!! God is calling you up higher!!!

Love,

Your new friend in Christ, Alex

Have you accepted Jesus Christ as your Savior?

> *That if you confess with your mouth, "Jesus is Lord," and believe in your heart that God raised him from the dead, you will be saved." For it is with your heart that you believe and are justified, and it is with your mouth that you confess and are saved. Romans 10:9-10*

I pray that if you did not know Jesus as your savior when you began this book, that you now have a deep desire to believe in Him and follow Him. The only way you will ever experience true fulfillment, is when you allow Jesus into your life to fulfill every aspect of it!

If you want to accept Jesus into your life, pray this prayer with a sincere heart:

"Dear Lord, I believe that you sent your son, Jesus, to die on the cross for my sins and he rose again 3 days later. I don't want to do things my way anymore, I want to follow you. Please forgive me for any and all sins that I've committed against you and make me a new creation! Today, I ask that you would come live inside of my heart. I ask and pray that you would baptize me in the holy spirit. Lead me to knowing you more and teach me how to follow you. In Jesus name, amen!"

Saying yes to Jesus will be the best decision you'll ever make in your entire life! Praise God for being a new creation in Christ!!! Now it's time for you to keep digging into the word and making time with God a daily habit!

Therefore if anyone is in Christ, he is a new creation; the old has gone, the new has come! 2 Corinthians 5:17

Alex Blackburn is a woman on fire for God. She has a deep passion to encourage and uplift people and to point them to Jesus. She has a burning desire in her heart to see captives set free and to see people walking in their God given talents and calling. Alex resides in NC with her beautiful daughter, Maliyah. Alex yearns to impact the world through speaking, writing, and any other outlet that the Lord has her use.

Go to the link below to stay updated on books, journals, and videos by Alex Blackburn:

https://linktr.ee/alexandriacb